ALSO BY JOSHUA DAVIS

Entrenched

The Underdog

SPARE PARTS

SPARE PARTS

FOUR UNDOCUMENTED TEENAGERS, ONE UGLY ROBOT, AND THE BATTLE FOR THE AMERICAN DREAM

JOSHUA DAVIS

FARRAR, STRAUS AND GIROUX
NEW YORK

Farrar, Straus and Giroux
18 West 18th Street, New York 10011

Printed in the United States of America
Published simultaneously in hardcover and paperback
First edition, 2014

Library of Congress Cataloging-in-Publication Data
Davis, Joshua, 1974–
    Spare parts : four undocumented teenagers, one ugly robot, and the
battle for the American dream / Joshua Davis. — First edition.
        pages   cm
    ISBN 978-0-374-18337-0 (hardcover) — ISBN 978-0-374-53498-1 (pbk.) —
ISBN 978-0-374-71265-5 (ebook)
    1. Robotics—Competitions—United States.   2. Remote
submersibles—Competitions—United States.   3. Mexican American
boys—Education—United States.   4. Mexican Americans—Economic
conditions.   5. Phoenix (Ariz.)—Social life and customs.   I. Title.

TJ211.26 .D38 2014
629.8'9207973—dc23

                                                      2014018569

Designed by Abby Kagan

Farrar, Straus and Giroux books may be purchased for educational, business, or
promotional use. For information on bulk purchases, please contact the Macmillan
Corporate and Premium Sales Department at 1-800-221-7945, extension 5442, or
write to specialmarkets@macmillan.com.

www.fsgbooks.com • www.fsgoriginals.com
www.twitter.com/fsgbooks • www.facebook.com/fsgbooks

5   7   9   10   8   6

For Allan Cameron, Fredi Lajvardi,
and America's teachers,
all of whom are on the front lines
of the American Dream

This is an exploration mission. Exploration means discovery of the new—and the unexpected. This competition will push your imagination and technical skills. Enter the event with the spirit of the men and women explorers who have set out into the unknown.

—2004 MARINE ADVANCED TECHNOLOGY EDUCATION
ROV COMPETITION DESIGN
AND BUILDING SPECIFICATIONS

CONTENTS

ON NOVEMBER 1, 2004, I received an e-mail from Marcos Garcíaacosta, an account manager at Intel in Chandler, Arizona. It looked like spam to me. The note began with the title "Robotics Team," then listed the address of a high school in Phoenix, some phone numbers, and a fax number. Jammed in there were the barely discernible words "Press Release."

"I thought you may be interested in this [*sic*] guys building robots, competing, and winning," Garcíaacosta wrote.

I was baffled.

My finger moved toward the delete button, but I hesitated. The e-mail went on to describe the extraordinary accomplishments of a small robotics team from an impoverished neighborhood in West Phoenix. Garcíaacosta explained that the team had never competed before—this was their rookie year—and yet they had achieved extraordinary success.

My first reaction was doubt. If they were so great, why hadn't I heard about them? The note seemed to be just another over-hyped press release. As a longtime writer for *Wired*, I receive breathless announcements every day. They trumpet amazing breakthroughs and life-changing trade shows. I press delete quickly.

But something about this press release was odd. The formatting was a mess and there were grammatical errors. And why was it coming from an account manager at Intel and not a publicist? I wasn't 100 percent sure I wanted to delete it, so I left it there and moved on with my day.

Over the next month, every time I got a standard, nicely formatted press release, it made me think of that unusual note. Finally, after four weeks, I realized I wasn't going to stop thinking about it. I pulled up the note, called the school, and asked to speak to the teacher in charge of the robotics team. I ended up on the phone with a man named Fredi Lajvardi.

I could hear kids talking in the background and the thump-thump-thump of some kind of electronic music. Fredi explained that his students were in the midst of building a new robot, but he was excited to talk. Over the summer, a local TV station had aired a segment about the school's success, but nobody seemed to pay attention. I was the first national journalist to call.

"When there's a fight or something, the press is all over us," he said. "We do something good, nobody pays attention."

The last time they had a brawl at the school, he told me, his students piloted a small, homemade robot past the news crew that had arrived. When that elicited little response, they drove circles around the camera. That prompted a few questions, but the crew largely ignored them. The journalists were there to talk about thugs, not robots.

I was intrigued. "So just back up a bit. How did your kids end up in an underwater-robotics competition?"

Fredi chuckled. "You're skeptical, right? So were the judges."

SPARE PARTS

TOM SWEAN eyed the four teenagers standing nervously at the front of the classroom. The kids were backed by a green chalkboard, and a swarm of desks crowded the space between them and the three judges. Swean was a gruff fifty-eight-year-old who ran the Navy's Ocean Engineering and Marine Systems program. At the Office of Naval Research he developed million-dollar autonomous, underwater robots for the SEALs. He was not used to dealing with Mexican American kids sporting gold chains, fake diamond rings, and patchy, adolescent mustaches.

"How'd you make the laser range-finder work?" Swean growled.

It was June 25, 2004—a hazy summer day at the University of California, Santa Barbara—and though the campus was largely empty due to the summer break, South Hall was crowded. It was the third annual Marine Advanced Technology Education Remotely Operated Vehicle Competition, an event sponsored by NASA and the Navy. It was established to encourage and identify the country's top engineering talent. There were teams from across the country, including students from MIT, who were sponsored by ExxonMobil, the world's largest publicly traded company. The Latino kids were from Carl Hayden Community High School in West Phoenix.

"We used a helium-neon laser," Cristian Arcega answered rapidly, keyed up on adrenaline. He was a skinny, five-foot-two science ace, one of the few nerds at Carl Hayden, a school where 71.17 percent of students received free or subsidized lunches because they were below the poverty line. Cristian lived in an eight-foot-by-eight-foot plywood box slapped onto the side of a trailer in a mobile-home park. "We captured its readout with a CCD camera and manually corrected by thirty percent to account for the index of refraction," Cristian explained to the judges.

Swean raised a bushy, graying eyebrow.

Lisa Spence, the flight lead at NASA's Neutral Buoyancy Laboratory, sat beside Swean. At NASA, she was in charge of replicating the space station in a 6.2-million-gallon tank at the Johnson Space Center in Houston, Texas. She had been at NASA for seventeen years and had worked with some of the most advanced underwater ROVs (remotely operated vehicles) in the world. Before starting at NASA, she had majored in chemical engineering at Arizona State University in the seventies and knew the area of Phoenix where these kids lived.

It wasn't a positive association. She remembered West Phoenix as a place that she wouldn't drive through by herself. It was a poor area and the better schools were elsewhere. So she was surprised to see an underwater-robotics team coming out of that neighborhood.

"There aren't oceans in Phoenix," she pointed out diplomatically.

"No, ma'am," Lorenzo Santillan said. "But we got pools."

Spence couldn't help but smile a little. Many of the teams had arrived at the competition with extraordinary underwater machines. They were made of machined metal, and some teams had budgets of more than ten thousand dollars. These kids had shown up with a garishly painted plastic robot that was partially assembled from scrap parts. They called their creation Stinky because it smelled so bad when they glued it together. It was their first time participating in any kind of underwater-robotics competition, but they had entered the highest division, going up against a field thick with veteran college teams. To some, their presence here seemed like a mistake.

But Lorenzo was clearly proud of the contraption. To him, it was a major accomplishment. He was fifteen years old and wore the back of his hair long so it fell past his shoulders. Kids in his neighborhood referred to it as the Mexican mullet. He'd been a member of the WBP gang before joining the robotics team, and he tried to walk with a tough guy's swagger. In reality, he was desperately trying to build a life outside the troubled world he'd grown up in.

Swean followed up with a question on signal interference, and Lorenzo looked at Oscar Vazquez, the team's de facto leader. Oscar was seventeen years old and sported the crew cut of an Army Ranger. For four years, he had distinguished himself as part of Carl Hayden's Junior Reserve Officer Training Corps, eventually becoming the group's executive officer. The previous year, the corps designated him Officer of the Year, the unit's highest honor. He dreamed of being a soldier, and it had looked as if he had a bright future in the military.

But it turned out the Army didn't want him. He had lived in Phoenix for six years and thought of himself as an American, even though he'd been born in Mexico. His parents had snuck him into Arizona when he was twelve. No matter how many push-ups he did or how fast he ran, he couldn't outpace the fact that he was a fugitive, living in the country illegally, and therefore barred from enlisting. When he realized this during his senior year, he went looking for another field in which to distinguish himself.

"Sir, we experimented with a fifteen-meter cable and found very low levels of interference," Oscar told Swean. "So we decided to extend our tether to thirty-three meters."

"You're very comfortable with the metric system," Swean observed.

"I grew up in Mexico, sir," Oscar said.

Swean nodded. He didn't care where the kids were from as long as they were smart. He eyed their rudimentary flip chart. "Why don't you have a PowerPoint display?"

"PowerPoint is a distraction," Cristian replied. "People use it when they don't know what to say."

"And you know what to say?"

"Yes, sir."

Spence knew that teams sometimes had an Einstein, Jr., a single kid who knew all the answers. Cristian clearly qualified, but Lorenzo and Oscar had also been able to speak intelligently about their robot's mechanical and electronic components. It was meant to be a team effort, so the judges took into account whether all team members could answer questions. Their robot had to successfully complete a complex series of underwater tasks, but about half the competition score would be based on this technical evaluation. Spence looked at Luis Aranda, a six-foot, 250-pound hulk of a kid who looked like Chief from *One Flew Over the Cuckoo's Nest*. He hadn't said anything yet.

"You employed PWM," she said, pointedly addressing Luis. "Can you describe that?"

Oscar, Cristian, and Lorenzo glanced at Luis. Throughout high school, he'd worked nights as a short-order cook at a diner and often seemed half-asleep during the day. They'd recruited him onto the team in part because they needed someone strong enough to lift the robot in and out of the pool. He rarely said much of anything, so it was hard to tell what he was thinking. Cristian wanted to answer for him but held back.

"PWM means 'pulse-width modulation,'" Luis answered, looking completely unfazed by the attention. "It's a technique for controlling high-current devices digitally."

Cristian couldn't believe it: the answer was spot-on. He wanted to hug the big guy.

Spence nodded. She would never have guessed that a down-trodden West Phoenix high school would have produced such an assured group of underwater roboticists. As a NASA employee, she had become accustomed to working with engineers who conformed to a sort of industry standard: white, well educated, conservative clothes. These four teenagers standing in front of her signaled that the future looked different.

ONE

LORENZO SANTILLAN had always been different. It might have been his head. When he was a few months old, his mother dropped him on a curb in Zitácuaro, a town of about 100,000 people in the Mexican state of Michoacán. He already had an odd, pear-shaped head, but now he developed a lump on his forehead. Laura Alicia Santillan was worried. She decided that he needed better medical attention than he was getting in Mexico, so she began the long journey to the United States, eventually slinking through a tunnel under the border with Lorenzo in 1988. Lorenzo was nine months old. She was motivated by a simple desire.

"We came to the U.S. to fix his head," she says.

She found a doctor in Phoenix who agreed to examine her son. The man said that surgery could realign Lorenzo's skull, but with a significant risk of brain damage. But, as far as the doctor could tell, Lorenzo was doing fine. The surgery would be strictly cosmetic and was otherwise unnecessary. Laura took another look at the bump above her son's right eyebrow and saw it in a new light. From that moment on, she told Lorenzo that the bump meant he was smart. "Your extra brains are in there," she told her son.

Now that Laura and Lorenzo were in the United States, there were reasons to stay. The family had barely been getting by in Mexico. After slicing off half of his right index finger in a carpentry accident, Pablo Santillan, Lorenzo's father, fed the family by disappearing into the forest for days on end with an ancient musket. He would return with skunks, squirrels, and iguanas slung over his shoulder. Laura dumped them into a stew, added some tomato, chili, and onion, and called it dinner. She was only four-teen when she married Pablo (he was twenty), and neither had made it past sixth grade. There weren't a lot of opportunities in Zitácuaro, but in the United States, Pablo had a shot at making five dollars an hour as a gardener. It seemed worth relocating.

The family moved into a two-room apartment near downtown Phoenix. A block away, prostitutes offered their services from an abandoned building. Drug dealers worked the corners. It was starkly different from Zitácuaro, where Pablo could search the forest for food. Now they lived in the middle of a big city and it wasn't possible to hunt for dinner. Laura got intermittent work as a hotel maid, and Pablo worked landscaping jobs throughout the scorching Arizona summer.

Before coming to the United States, Laura had given birth to two children: Lorenzo and his older brother, Jose. When she crossed over to the United States, she was pregnant and soon gave birth to Pablo, Jr., on U.S. soil, which meant that her third child became an American citizen. Yoliet and Fernando, a daugh-ter and a son, were also born in the United States. The three American-born siblings would go on to have significantly more opportunities to live and work in the United States than the two who had adopted the country as their new home.

For Laura, Mexico soon became "an erased memory." But Pablo never forgot the solitude of the Mexican forest. A quiet, stoic man, he wore cowboy boots and sported a handlebar mus-tache so thick, it hid his mouth. He had the hard-drinking, soli-tary nature of a cowboy but now found himself in a vast urban desert with five children. It was a heavy load to bear. At night and on weekends, he often bought a twelve-pack of Milwaukee's Best and started working his way through it. As Lorenzo tells it, when Pablo was drunk, he became emotional. Sometimes he told Lorenzo that he loved him, other times he snapped. On one occasion, when Lorenzo was in middle school, Pablo asked his son to clean up the living room. When Lorenzo refused, Pablo grabbed an electrical extension cord and went after him.

School wasn't much better. As Lorenzo got older, his jowls bulged out but the top of his head stayed comparatively narrow, giving it an egg shape. Kids mocked him for his misshapen head and, once he got to middle school, they laughed at his unibrow. "I didn't understand why people would do that," Lorenzo says. Many days, he came home crying.

With little choice, Lorenzo decided to embrace the fact that he was different. While the other kids at school had short hair and nice fades, Lorenzo went the other way. His mother cut his hair—they couldn't afford a barber—so he asked her to only trim his bangs and let the rest of his hair grow out. Soon, he had a mullet.

"It looks really nice," Laura told her son.

His classmates were less supportive; the ridicule was frequent and varied. Sometimes they called him an egghead; other times, he was referred to as El Buki, after a long-haired Mexican pop singer. When students called him a woman, he fired back that he was more of a man because he could take all the insults. "I don't want to be like everyone else!" he yelled back, and tried to pretend it didn't hurt.

In seventh grade, a friend asked him to carry marijuana for Sur Trece, a local gang associated with the Crips. He agreed and was entrusted with a pound of weed, which he stashed in his backpack. Eventually, he was instructed to leave it in a hole on school grounds. He did as he was told but was terrified the whole time. "I could get my ass kicked at any moment," he kept thinking. He realized he wasn't cut out to be a criminal and refused to do it again.

Instead, when he arrived as a freshman at Carl Hayden Community High School, he decided to join the marching band. To prepare him, his mother found a piano program offered by the Salvation Army and managed to get a free upright piano (though it was missing a number of keys). She set it up on the back patio so he could practice. Lorenzo learned how to play pieces by Debussy ("Clair de lune"), Erik Satie (Gymnopédie no. 3), and Chopin (Sonata no. 2). Lorenzo could listen to the music a few times and then play it back. He figured he was learning enough that he could wing it at band practice.

Unfortunately, band practice is not a place where winging it works. The first problem was that the band had no piano. The closest thing the music teacher could come up with was the xylophone. Next, Lorenzo had no idea what to play since he couldn't read the sheet music.

Nonetheless, as Christmas neared, the teacher handed him a uniform and hat and told him to get ready for the annual holiday parade. Lorenzo dutifully donned the outfit, strapped the hulking xylophone to his body, and marched alongside the rest of the band as they paraded down Central Avenue in downtown Phoenix. He knew the songs they were performing had big parts for the xylophone, but he couldn't play them. Every now and then he would try to hit a few notes, but they were always wrong. As the parade streamed endlessly through downtown Phoenix, he kept wondering when the humiliation would be over. The best he could do was keep his legs in time with the others as they walked.

"It was a walk of shame," he says.

He returned the xylophone and never went back to band. He felt that he didn't belong anywhere, though he was desperate to find friends, or at least people who wouldn't mock him. But it was high school and he looked funny. He had also been held back a year in first grade when he was still learning English. As a result, he was a year older than his classmates, which suggested he had flunked a grade.

Lorenzo tried to reason with his hecklers. When he mispronounced a word in English and kids laughed, he pleaded for some sympathy: "Why you gotta make fun of me for something I meant?" That only produced more laughter.

Lorenzo's anger mounted and he started picking fights at school. He ended up bruised, scraped, and in the principal's office. He was on track to be expelled. In an effort to turn him around, the school counselor assigned him to anger-management class. He learned that his anger was explosive, the most dangerous type. If he didn't rein it in, he would self-destruct. The counselor showed him how to calm himself by counting backward from ten. The problem was, he wasn't sure he wanted to calm himself. It was hard to ignore all the teasing.

After school, Lorenzo started helping his godfather fix cars. Hugo Ceballos lived with the Santillan family and had set up an informal business in their driveway; anybody with car problems could pull in and Hugo would pop the hood, figure out what was wrong, and fix it right there.

Hugo wouldn't let Lorenzo do much more than clean the tools with a rag damp with gasoline. It gave Lorenzo an excuse to stand beside the cars and watch. He learned that when you jack up a car, you should position a tire on the ground beside you when you slide under the vehicle. That way, if the jack fails, the car will land on the tire, not you.

That's a badass idea, Lorenzo thought.

Lorenzo wanted to do more, but Hugo didn't let him. So Lorenzo hovered on the periphery, cleaning the occasional tool and watching closely as Jose, his older brother, helped. Hugo explained to Jose that it was important to keep track of all your parts. "Anything you take off a car, remember where it goes," he told Lorenzo's brother. When Hugo installed a rebuilt engine, Lorenzo stood a few feet back and listened as Hugo showed Jose how to use a torque wrench to tighten the bolts. Lorenzo listened carefully and tried to get as close as he could to the car. He had to be careful though; if he got in Hugo's or Jose's way, he'd get yelled at and told to go inside.

The chief lesson Lorenzo learned was that it was important to be creative. Hugo wasn't running a normal mechanic's shop, with a wall full of tools and shelves filled with supplies. He had little money, a small set of hand tools, and his ingenuity. To survive, he had to come up with fresh ideas and adapt.

Lorenzo took that to heart. He didn't fit into white American culture and couldn't find his place in the immigrant community. Even band—the standard home for high school misfits—didn't work for him. But his days looking over Hugo's shoulder in the driveway had taught him to think outside the norm. In the driveway, an unusual idea wasn't necessarily bad. In fact, it might be the only solution.

AT ONE TIME, Carl Hayden was a well-regarded school; it even had its own off-site equestrian program. Students could ride horses in an indoor facility so they wouldn't get too hot in the desert heat. The school district even built a rodeo ring for teens. It was meant to be a school for white kids.

It's not that way anymore. Now the neighborhood around the school has an abandoned, overlooked feel. Some of the roads are still unpaved dirt. Junk-food wrappers and diapers lie in the desiccated weeds on the side of the road. At the school entrance on West Roosevelt, security guards, two squad cars, and a handful of cops watch teenagers file past a sign that reads, CARL HAYDEN COMMUNITY HIGH SCHOOL: THE PRIDE'S INSIDE.

There certainly isn't a lot of pride on the outside. The school buildings are mostly drab, late-1950s-era boxes. The front lawn is nothing but brown scrub and patches of dirt. The class photos beside the principal's office tell the story of the past four decades. In 1965, the students were nearly all white, wearing blazers, ties, and long skirts. Now the school is 92 percent Hispanic. Drooping, baggy shorts and crisply ironed denim shirts are the norm.

The current student body reflects the transformation of Phoenix. The city was founded in 1868 by Jack Swilling, a morphine-addicted former Confederate officer. Swilling had come to Arizona seeking gold but ended up falling in love with a Mexican woman instead. Trinidad Mejia Escalante, a seventeen-year-old from Hermosillo, Mexico, was visiting relatives in southern Arizona when she encountered Swilling. Escalante's mother didn't approve of the drug-addled soldier, but the young lady was smitten and eloped.

Soon after their marriage, the Swillings built a canal near the Salt River, a meager flow of water that spills out of the burnt-umber Mazatzal Mountains into a broad, flat valley. They planted corn, sorghum, and even a vineyard and discovered that the land was productive. The winters were warm and the soil rich. Before long, the Swilling Canal drew other settlers, one of whom dubbed the new community Phoenix. This referred to the ancient, ruined Indian canals that still ran across the land, the remnants of a lost civilization that was now rising again as a result of the marriage of an American man and Mexican woman.

In 1870, early Anglo immigrants to the region named the town's east–west streets after U.S. presidents and labeled the north–south roads by local Indian-tribe names. It seemed like a fitting compromise, given the history of the region. But in 1893, the town council decided that the Indian names were too hard to remember and renamed the north–south roads with numbers. The new names also helped Anglo immigrants feel that the land was more fully theirs.

As the city developed, tax revenue was largely allocated to infrastructure for the neighborhoods settled by Anglos. The white neighborhoods got water lines, sewage pipes, and paved roads. The barrios where Mexican immigrants settled got almost nothing. In 1891, the Phoenix Chamber of Commerce published a pamphlet touting their achievements. "Here are none of the sleepy, semi-Mexican features of the more ancient towns of the Southwest, but, in the midst of a valley of wonderful fertility, has risen a city of stately structures, beautiful homes, progressive and vigorous."

When World War Two brought a boom in wartime manufacturing, factories were opened in West Phoenix, away from the pretty citrus groves and canals of East Phoenix. To house workers, companies such as Goodyear and Alcoa constructed small villages near their factories. The housing attracted working-class whites, who built a community in the area. Carl Hayden Community High School was meant to serve that population.

But in the sixties and seventies, as the factories expanded and pollution increased, the working-class whites in West Phoenix migrated out of the area. Leukemia outbreaks among children were reported. In many cases, the housing was poorly built, as it was meant to be only temporary. "Anybody who could afford it moved to the East Side," says John Jaquemart, a historian for the City of Phoenix, who grew up in East Phoenix during that time. "At the least, you moved somewhere else."

At the same time, the population of the region was exploding, driven by a boom in agriculture and high-tech industries. In 1950, the city had 106,818 residents, making it the ninety-ninth-largest city in the United States. Over the next ten years, the population quadrupled and added hundreds of thousands of residents every decade after that. By 1990, Phoenix had a population of almost a million people and was the sixth-largest city in the United States.

The population boom led to a ripple effect across the region's economy as relatively wealthy, newly arrived residents needed a variety of services, from landscaping to cleaning. The spike in demand for labor was met in part by immigrants who streamed across the border illegally, all of whom needed somewhere to stay. West Phoenix was the prime choice. It was cheap and close to downtown, and whites were abandoning it because of the potential health problems and poorly built, decades-old temporary homes.

The changing demographics of the city posed a challenge for school administrators. A 1974 Supreme Court ruling prohibited busing between districts, which meant that white people in the suburbs could stay in their own schools, while minorities in the city center were left with the facilities abandoned by their predecessors. Nonetheless, in 1985 a federal judge ordered the district to desegregate. With few options, administrators tried to entice white students into the inner city. In the mid-1980s, Carl Hayden became a magnet specializing in marine science and computer programming. The thinking ran roughly along these lines: white people like the ocean and computers, so if there's a school that offers specialized classes focused on those things, it'll attract white people.

It didn't work. No amount of computer programming or oceanography curriculum was enough to entice white families, who fled to the suburban neighborhoods surrounding Phoenix. While tony districts such as Scottsdale and Mesa filled with white students, Phoenix grew increasingly Hispanic. Finally, the district just gave up. There was no more diversity to balance. In 2004, Carl Hayden was 98 percent Hispanic—pretty much all the white kids had left—so in 2005, the federal court lifted its two-decade-old desegregation order. Administrators and some teachers tried to put a sunny spin on it. "From school to school, we are equally balanced," announced Shirley Filliater-Torres, the president of the district's Classroom Teachers Association. She didn't point out that the schools were equally balanced because they were nearly completely filled with one race. "We have probably done as good a job as we can to desegregate, given our student population," she said.

The transformation was complete. West Phoenix was Hispanic. And while that population worked downtown or in East Phoenix—cleaning the city at night like ghosts that disappeared at sunrise—the doctors and engineers in Scottsdale and Mesa rarely ventured west. Various reasons were given: it was dangerous, it was dirty, it was hot.

"We looked with nothing but contempt at anything west of Central Avenue," says William Collins, a historian with the Arizona State Historic Preservation Office.

According to Jaquemart, the City of Phoenix historian, East

Siders claimed they could never live on the West Side because the sun would be in their eyes as they drove downtown to work in the morning. Jaquemart's geography professor at ASU put it more succinctly:

"There's nothing worthwhile there."

CRISTIAN ARCEGA TRIED not to care about what others thought of him since it usually wasn't positive. As a young boy growing up in Mexicali, Mexico, he was short and skinny and didn't excel at the things that usually got you noticed. He wasn't good at cracking jokes and couldn't play soccer without tripping over his own feet. His diminutive size made him easy to push around. He quickly realized that it was more interesting to stay inside, away from bullies, and play with things that didn't try to hurt him.

Except sometimes they did. When he was four years old, Cristian disassembled the family radio and snapped a few internal wires with a fork. Then he plugged the disemboweled device back in. He was curious to see what would happen if he broke connections and then electrified the whole thing. When he flipped the switch, the radio popped with a bright electric flash and the lights in the house went out. His mother rushed in and grabbed him. As she yelled at him, he could only think one thing: "Wow, that was fun."

Soon, anything his mother bought him ended up in pieces on the concrete floor of their unfinished home in an impoverished neighborhood near the U.S. border. "He always wanted to get on the inside of everything," his mother recalls.

When he turned five, he announced that he wanted to build robots. Nobody in the family knew what to say. He attended a kindergarten made out of wooden shipping pallets; there wasn't a lot of technology in the classroom. Nor had he gotten the idea from his parents, who hadn't finished elementary school and had little interest in programmable machines. But somehow Cristian had become obsessed with building robots.

In 1994, Juan Arcega, Cristian's father, traveled to the United States and found work in Arizona fabricating mobile storage containers. Juan made more than he was making in Mexicali in a vegetable-packing factory, but he missed his family. Plus, he felt that the United States offered more opportunities for his unusual son. Cristian kept trying to build things out of lumber scraps and rusted nails—from helicopters that wouldn't fly to race cars that barely rolled—and Juan was pretty sure that Cristian wasn't going to get a chance to improve his skills if he stayed in Mexicali. In the United States, he might have a chance.

In November 1995, members of Cristian's family drove him across the border. He was five years old, and the journey felt like a mystery, largely because he fell asleep in the car. When he woke up, he was in Yuma, Arizona. His family said nothing about the crossing. They just kept driving another two hours east until they reached the small town of Stanfield, Arizona.

Stanfield didn't seem like much of a step up from Mexicali. It had a population of about six hundred people but felt like a ghost town. Tumbleweeds blew through vacant lots. Of the homes that did exist, many were boarded up. The town featured a few dollops of green farmland in the midst of the vast, empty Sonoran Desert.

The Arcegas moved into the home that Juan had rented. Cristian remembers it as "a scary-looking, decrepit house" with torn-up shutters and holes in the walls. Luckily it didn't rain much, because the roof was full of holes. They lived there with another family, all packed together in three dusty rooms.

Cristian started school that December at Stanfield Elementary. The campus was a collection of cute brick buildings with a sign out front featuring a roadrunner, the school's mascot. It seemed like a nice place, except that Cristian couldn't speak any English. On his first day, he sat down at a fake-wood-laminated desk with a cubbyhole beneath it. As the third-grade teacher chattered away incomprehensibly, Cristian watched the other students pull worksheets from the desks. He did the same but couldn't make sense of the English instructions. He looked over at a girl sitting beside him, but she said something sharp and covered up her work.

At the end of the day, he was supposed to take the school bus home. His mother had told him which bus to take, but when he walked out to find it, he was confronted with an array of identical-looking yellow buses. He saw a girl he recognized—he had seen her playing at a house near him—so he followed her onto a bus.

The bus drove and drove. Nothing looked familiar. When the girl got off, Cristian didn't see his house anywhere so he didn't move. Finally, he fell asleep. He was awoken by the driver and saw that he was the only kid left on the bus. It was dark out. He had been on the bus for hours.

"Where do you live?" the man asked.

Cristian showed him a slip of paper. His mother had written out the address. The guy laughed and said something. Cristian got the gist: "You got on the really wrong bus, kid."

The guy was nice about it and went out of his way to drive Cristian home. But as the school year progressed, Cristian kept having trouble. Sometimes he'd end up a quarter of the way to Yuma; other times, he'd be halfway to Phoenix before he realized there was a problem. He'd watch one child after the other get off until he was the last kid on board. He coped by falling asleep. On at least one occasion, his mother went to the school when he didn't show up for dinner, and an administrator radioed the buses until a driver reported that one sleeping boy was on board.

He was assigned to an English-learner program but continued to be mystified. One day, when he couldn't understand an assignment, one of his teachers yelled at him. Cristian could read all the words; he just didn't know what they meant. He received straight Fs that year.

Some of the kids weren't welcoming. He remembers hearing the word *wetback* for the first time on the school bus. It was directed at him. Kids felt bolder on the bus because the bus driver was driving and couldn't do anything to stop the taunting. Most of the time Cristian couldn't exactly tell what the kids were saying to him, but he knew it wasn't nice.

Obviously he wouldn't win a fight. He was small, and outnumbered. But he was also unwilling to give in. Though he was ridiculed by some of his teachers and taunted by his classmates, Cristian was convinced, even by age six, that he was smarter than most of them. His smug detachment only ratcheted up the abuse. One boy in particular seemed to take pleasure in calling Cristian names. Finally, on the last day of the school year, as Cristian was walking off the bus, he smashed his fist into one kid's face and fled to his house before anybody could respond.

That summer, the family moved to a trailer on the outskirts of town as temperatures rocketed up to 110 degrees. When Cristian ventured outside to play in the dirt, it burned his hands. When he grabbed a piece of metal to make something, it singed his skin and left a welt. After that, he decided to just stay indoors. They had a television and could sometimes pick up a static-filled transmission of Spanish-language *Power Rangers* from Nogales, about a hundred miles to the south.

That's when he flipped onto an American broadcast of a bearded white guy wielding a circular saw. The man had gray hair and a slightly nasal voice and was tearing through a piece of wood with the saw. Cristian quickly realized that the man was building a staircase. His younger sister complained—she wanted to watch cartoons—but Cristian refused to let her change the channel. He had just discovered the magic of Bob Vila, home-improvement guru extraordinaire.

From 1979 until 2007, Vila hosted a series of popular fix-up-your-home shows, helping to touch off a home-remodeling craze and inspiring Tim Allen's comedy show *Home Improvement*.

With a flat American accent, plaid shirts, and a New England–based remodeling business, Vila came across as an old-time Yankee. In reality, he was born in Cuba. His family had fled Havana in 1944 and he'd grown up in a Spanish-speaking family in Miami.

"At some point you have to consciously choose your identity, and I chose to be an American kid," Vila says of growing up in a Spanish-speaking family. "For the next forty-eight years, I didn't focus on my heritage."

And yet in 1996, in a trailer out in the middle of the Arizona desert, Vila became a symbol of hope for a young boy struggling with his own cultural identity. Vila and the machines he used mesmerized Cristian. The six-year-old boy didn't need to speak English to appreciate the raw beauty of a cement mixer or the twisted innards of an air compressor. He just loved watching the power tools, and how they made the sawdust fly. Vila's table saw looked enormous, like something a giant would use. It was a glimpse into a magical world, where people had an endless amount of building supplies and extraordinary tools. Cartoons paled in comparison. For Cristian, Bob Vila's *Home Again* was the real fairy tale.

It was thrilling to watch but also frustrating. The lot next door was filled with old cars. Untold mechanical riches were just on the other side of a chain-link fence, but the guy who owned the property refused to let Cristian examine the cars. He even accused Cristian of stealing parts. Cristian responded that the cars were nothing but junk; nobody would want them.

Every year, Cristian looked forward to the monsoon season, which typically began around June. The wind would pick up and whip massive plumes of dust thousands of feet into the sky. It blotted out the sun and made things cooler, but that wasn't the best part. What Cristian liked most was the strange variety of things that would blow into his yard, from geometrically complex tumbleweeds to basketballs, which could be used to make models of the solar system. He remembers watching a twelve-foot plastic swimming pool spin down out of the sky and land in front of his house. It was the closest he could get to the bounty of Bob Vila's show.

When he was nine years old, the family moved to a run-down trailer park in West Phoenix. Juan had gotten a job as a welder at a company that fabricated metal ramps for disabled people. Ironically, one client turned out to be the Border Patrol. Juan's family was in the United States illegally, but he was nonetheless dispatched to Nogales to install access ramps at Border Patrol facilities.

The trailer park was called Catalina Village and billed itself as a "walled community." Long stretches of the five-foot cinderblock wall surrounding it were unpainted except the portions that had been graffitied and then hastily covered with whatever paint was on hand. The entrance featured a prominent sign that stated NO LOUD MUSIC in both English and Spanish. A pair of tennis shoes hung on electrical wires over the entrance, signaling that drugs could be bought in the vicinity. The park's website put a cheery spin on the situation: "Start living the time of your life in one of our Phoenix, Arizona, homes!"

The Arcegas moved into a pink single-wide trailer. It felt like a huge step up to Cristian, mainly because there wasn't dirt everywhere. He was also just a block away from Alta Butler Elementary School. That meant no more school buses and fewer chances that he'd be taunted. He could simply walk to school.

The downside was that he developed allergies. His sinuses clogged and his eyes watered. His mother took him to a doctor, who tested a variety of allergens on his skin and concluded that Cristian was allergic to nearly everything. His mother decided that the best (and most affordable) solution was for Cristian to stay indoors and watch more television.

He soon found that watching Bob Vila had improved his English. By fourth grade, he was fluent, and by fifth grade, he was getting straight As. He was so adept, he found himself wondering why everyone else in his class was so slow. "All of a sudden it was boring," he says.

He spent as much time as he could in the school's meager library, reading through the most challenging books he could find. He quickly ran out of options and found himself disgusted by a National Geographic series for kids that was low on facts and information. He also decided that schoolwork was inane and beneath him, but he did it anyway. It was easier to get it done than it was to prove to his parents and teachers that it was all a useless exercise.

He didn't encounter a teacher who inspired him until eighth grade. Ms. Hildenbrandt taught chemistry and encouraged Cristian to choose an independent project that interested him. Cristian decided he wanted to study rocket science. In particular, he wanted to explore the effect that a variety of different fin designs had on the aerodynamic properties of a rocket. Hildenbrandt thought it was a great idea and told him to dive in.

Cristian recruited a couple of other students to be part of his launch team. Together they scrounged a few dollars and bought a model-rocket kit from a mail-order catalog. Then after school one day, Cristian tied heavy fishing line to one end of the soccer field fence and ran the line back about 160 yards to another fence. Kids were playing a game on the field, but he ran the string down the sideline. He figured it'd be okay.

When he pulled the string taut and affixed the rocket to it, he was excited. He had a perfect experiment. He had equipped the rocket with the smallest engine possible, and a series of calculations led him to believe that it wouldn't cover the entire distance between the fences. He would ignite the rocket, watch it zip horizontally along the string, and measure how far it flew. By testing out a series of fin designs, he'd determine which was the most aerodynamic based on how far the rocket traveled. That was the idea anyway.

He carefully inserted the electric igniters, paid out the wires, and, just for fun, started a countdown: "Three, two, one, blastoff!"

The rocket engine erupted with a roar and immediately melted the plastic fishing line. Now loosed from its guideline, the rocket was free to fly in any direction and was aimed horizontally across the playground. The kids playing soccer in the middle of the field screamed and dove for cover.

Almost instantaneously, the rocket pivoted, shot straight up into the air, and emitted a huge boom above the field. A teacher came tearing out of a classroom and saw terrified children scattering everywhere. Up above, the rocket was peacefully descending from the sky beneath a parachute. While everyone else kept their distance, one kid ran excitedly toward the rocket: Cristian.

"That's how they knew who did it," Cristian says.

The teacher chastised him and told him never to do something so reckless again. Cristian said he understood, and resigned himself to shelving the rocket. But privately, he was already wondering what his next experiment might be.

As eighth grade drew to an end, Cristian started thinking about high school. He had heard about the international baccalaureate program at North High School. It was supposed to be a lot of hard work and that appealed to him. But when he visited to get an application, he was told no spaces were available. Rather than look elsewhere, he decided that his neighborhood school would be fine. Carl Hayden was only six blocks away and boasted two interesting magnet programs: computer science and marine science. The programs may not have attracted a lot of white students, but they attracted Cristian.

When Cristian arrived at Carl Hayden, he decided to sign up for all honors courses, mainly so that he could insulate himself from "the idiots" who heckled the teachers, played pranks in class, and mocked his seriousness. He appreciated that honors students tended not to cause a ruckus, but he wasn't particularly impressed with their intelligence. He skipped freshman science and took sophomore biology instead.

He also tried to supplement his learning by researching cell biology and Shakespeare online. The problem was, the only Internet access he had at home was via a dial-up modem. He would just be getting into the juicy details of cell replication when his sister would pick up the phone and sever the connection. "Hey!" he'd yell. His sister yelled back that there were others in the family who needed to use the phone. She also accused him of being an adopted space alien their parents had found beside a garbage container.

Cristian's brief glimpses of a world filled with knowledge tantalized him. They also made school seem dull in comparison. It wasn't hard for him to excel. He quickly established himself as one of the top two students in his class of six hundred. But he was bored. Really, really bored.

That's when he met Fredi Lajvardi.

He could hear the Carl Hayden marine science magnet program before he saw it. Most days, the sound of a bass drum reverberated off the terrazzo hallway tiles and a techno song vibrated the air. The sound came from room 2134, a darkened, windowless classroom lined with fish tanks. Soft light emanated from the bubbling, glowing tanks, lending a sort of club atmosphere to the room. At first glance, it was hard to spot the teacher. That's because Fredi Lajvardi often hovered in the back, playing music off a series of computers. Known to his students as Ledge, a condensed and reimagined version of his Iranian last name, Fredi had the wiry energy of a DJ at an all-night dance party.

Technically, Fredi was the program manager of the marine-science program, a post he had held since 2001. In reality, he'd never been that interested in lecturing or teaching in any traditional way. At the beginning of every class, he convened "huddles" like a football coach, assigning kids individual missions for the period. "Okay, let's do this," he liked to enthuse, clapping his hands together and sending kids back to their tables. He doled out advice constantly: "Think about the moon's gravitational pull"; "You really going to leave that garbage on my floor?"; "If anybody hears a bomb threat, you tell me." His classroom had the high-intensity energy of a sporting event, where Fredi was the coach, cheerleader, band, mascot, janitor, and security detail, all rolled into one.

The music was an important part of the atmosphere. In fact, the techno thumping out of the speakers in Fredi's classroom was often his own. He recorded an album in the early 2000s— *Ledge on the Edge*—though he had never tried to sell it. He composed at night using ACIDPlanet audio software and played his tracks on an endless loop during the day for his captive audience. The reviews were mixed—Cristian personally thought it sounded awful—but the students weren't willing to openly criticize the teacher's tunes. Much of the music has the mid-eighties feel of the *Beverly Hills Cop* sound track—squeaky blips, pops, and bright, punchy rhythms—but by the fifth or sixth repeat of the music, it fades innocuously into the background.

The music still had an effect, even after students stopped listening. Its bright, driving rhythm signaled that there were a million things to be done. It was almost impossible to listen to it and sit still. On ACIDPlanet.com—a forum for users of the music software—Fredi laid out his aim: "I hope people play my music when they need to be energized and get going!"

On his drive into school in the morning, Fredi liked to blast his own music. It never seemed as if he needed any additional energy though. He was a wiry, bearded, five-foot-six-inch dynamo, brimming with the enthusiasm of a long-distance runner. In high school, he went to the state cross-country championship every year, laying down mid-five-minute miles in the 5K. Now in his forties, he managed sub-six-minute miles, pushing himself with the determination of someone who still had something to prove.

The music was part of his educational philosophy. Fredi had always focused on getting kids excited to learn. He cared less about covering the required curriculum and more about finding hands-on projects. To many students, school felt sterile and bureaucratic. Fredi's music was just one way he tried to change the ambience. It didn't necessarily matter if they liked it. It was enough to be different.

He also fought for unstructured time in the school day. When he arrived at Carl Hayden in 1987, he started a class called Science Seminar. There was no curriculum. Fredi just told students to find something fun to build or an idea to test. Over the years, students had embarked on a variety of unusual projects. One student tried to teach color-blind rats the differences among colors. Another student constructed a 1:60 clay model of downtown Phoenix, placed it in a wind tunnel, and blew carbon dioxide across it. The goal: determine how architecture could be used to increase air circulation and help dissipate trapped air pollution. Fredi's room became the refuge of tinkerers, inventors, and frustrated dreamers.

So when Cristian Arcega wandered into the marine science classroom one day, Fredi was primed to appreciate his talent. Cristian had heard about Fredi from Michael Hanck, a fellow freshman who was taking marine science. With Fredi's encouragement, Hanck had started building robots in the classroom.

"Robots?" Cristian asked Hanck.

It was what he'd been waiting his whole life to hear.

ON JULY 27, 1997, police in the Phoenix suburb of Chandler fanned out on foot and bicycles, in patrol cars and paddy wagons. They had received complaints from residents who were bothered by immigrants bathing naked in the orange groves around town. Other locals were upset that people assumed to be Mexicans were loitering around the Circle K on the corner of Arizona Avenue and Fairview Street. The problem took on global proportions in the mind of the authorities. James Dailey, an Immigration and Naturalization Service intelligence agent, described the area as "the first- or second-most notorious staging site for aliens in the world."

Agents quickly identified likely targets. When Venecia Robles Zavala, a mother of three young children, stepped out of the Food City on Arizona and Warner, a police officer on a bicycle stopped her. He overheard her arguing with her five-year-old in Spanish and demanded to see papers.

"What papers?" she asked, surprised. "Newspapers?"

"Immigration papers," the officer clarified.

"I'm an American citizen."

The officer asked her to prove it, so she showed him her driver's license. The man wasn't satisfied; a driver's license was not proof of citizenship. Given that he'd heard her speaking Spanish, he needed further confirmation. A passport or Social Security card would do. Luckily, she had her birth certificate in her trunk. It was enough to convince the officer that she shouldn't be deported.

Four hundred and thirty-two other "Hispanic-looking" people

were caught in a sweep that police labeled Operation Restoration. The stated goal was to "build stronger neighborhoods." On day six of the crackdown, police and Border Control "circled the wagons" at Hamilton High School and chased down thirteen "aliens." The immigrants were loaded into a van and deported. At a nearby Little Caesars, a sixteen-year-old and his friend were waiting for their pizza when a police officer and a Border Patrol agent entered and asked if they were "legal." The teenager said he was, but the officers didn't believe him. They instructed the staff to refund the boys' money—they weren't going to be eating pizza tonight—and loaded them into a squad car. One boy was able to call his mother, who arrived in the nick of time with her son's Social Security card, but his friend wasn't so lucky and was deported.

Agents were required to fill out form I-213—the Record of Deportable Alien—when they detained an immigrant. The form contained room for a description of the detained individual, in part to show that officers had probable cause for apprehending the person. According to INS paperwork related to the sweep, probable cause could be "clothing consistent with that of illegal entrant aliens" or "a strong body odor common to illegal aliens."

The police didn't restrict their activities to the street. On July 28, 1997, the authorities convinced a trailer-park manager to notate a map with Xs for every trailer that contained suspected illegal immigrants. At approximately 11:00 p.m. that night, officers banged on the door of a sleeping family. A man identified by police as B awoke to see bright lights shining through the windows. When he opened the door, the officers strode in, despite B's protests.

"We can do whatever we want," an officer responded, though he admitted that they didn't have warrants. "We are the Chandler Police Department. You have people who are here illegally."

B's four children were roused, as was his brother-in-law, and all were ordered to produce their papers. The police refused to allow them to change out of their pajamas, even after B showed the officers that two of his children were U.S. citizens, while he and his other two kids were legal residents. When officers discovered that B's brother-in-law had an expired visa, they radioed for backup and carted him away in his pajamas.

When the Arizona attorney general Grant Woods reviewed the roundup, he found that a pregnant woman had been loaded into a van with no windows and no water on a day when temperatures reached 101 degrees. "At the scene of one mass stop and arrest, canine units were called in by the Chandler Police which resulted in at least one individual being bitten by a dog," Woods noted in his report. He also pointed out that, in at least one case, a local cop had used "physical force beyond what appeared appropriate for the arrest" and needed to be restrained by the Border Patrol agents accompanying him. Woods also pointed out that most of the deportees had no criminal record: "There were no other warrants, charges, or holds for these individuals that in any way indicated other criminal activity or that required extraordinary security or physical force."

Woods wrote, "The issue raised by this type of treatment is not whether the arrest and deportation is legal, but whether human beings are entitled to some measure of dignity and safety even when they are suspected of being in the United States illegally."

While the Chandler raid was one of the largest in Phoenix history, it was not an isolated event. A raid in the Phoenix suburb of Mesa in December netted 191 illegal immigrants, and in March 2000, the INS nabbed another 140 suspected illegal immigrants in the area. In January of 2000, the INS launched Operation Denial, a task force of one hundred agents dispatched to Phoenix's Sky Harbor Airport and Las Vegas' McCarran International Airport. Phoenix was the prime focus—INS officials referred to Sky Harbor as the "Grand Central Station" of immigrant smuggling in the United States.

The climate in Arizona was rapidly deteriorating. In 2000, a rancher named Roger Barnett declared open season on migrants. "Humans, the greatest prey on earth," he told a London newspaper. He sewed a homemade PATRIOT PATROL patch on his shirt, mounted an ATV, and ranged across his twenty-two-thousand-acre Arizona ranch looking for anybody who appeared Mexican. According to court documents, when he found Hispanic-looking people on his land, he held them at gunpoint and threatened to kill them. His bravado inspired others, who formed armed vigilante groups to patrol the state.

In 2003, eighty miles south of Phoenix, twelve migrants were sleeping beside a cattle pond. They were waiting for a smuggler to guide them farther into the United States when two men dressed in camouflage appeared. The men were carrying an automatic rifle and a pistol and opened fire, killing two of the migrants. The police later found the bodies riddled with bullets. No one was apprehended for the crime.

By 2004, when Cristian arrived at Fredi's marine science classroom, organizations such as the Minutemen, Ranch Rescue, and American Border Patrol were scouring the state for illegal immigrants. "This is an invasion, the greatest invasion in history," wrote presidential hopeful Patrick J. Buchanan in his book *State of Emergency: The Third World Invasion and Conquest of America*. "What Mexico is doing to the American Southwest has, from time immemorial, been the way one tribe has slowly conquered and colonized the lands of another."

For Buchanan, it seemed, nothing less than the survival of the United States was at stake. Migrants who were seemingly coming to the United States to clean toilets and hammer nails were actually, from his perspective, hatching an insidious plot to recapture land Mexico lost during the 1846–48 Mexican-American War. The plot, he said, was named *La Reconquista*.

"*La Reconquista* is not to be accomplished by force of arms, as was the U.S. annexation of the Southwest and California in 1848," he wrote. "It is to be carried out by a nonviolent invasion and cultural transformation of that huge slice of America into a Mexamerican border-land, where the dominant culture is Hispanic and Anglos will feel alienated and begin to emigrate."

A key element in this purported plot were migrant children. Buchanan argued that families came to the United States to leech off government services. They weren't here to work; they were here to apply for welfare. School was a thorny issue. He accepted the idea that immigrant children wanted to attend school—and might therefore want to assimilate and contribute to the country—but he argued that it was a bad idea to educate them, as it overtaxed the education system and drained resources from long-standing citizens. It was better, in Buchanan's view, to turn them away, particularly since he believed they would never amount to much: "Millions of immigrants, but especially their children, who today survive on welfare are being inculcated with the values of a subculture of gangs, crime, drugs, and violence."

Buchanan may have just been a pundit with lofty aspirations, but Joe Arpaio, the sheriff of Maricopa County, agreed with Buchanan, and though just as vocal, he wields real authority. Sheriff Joe, as he's known locally, has had jurisdiction over the city of Phoenix and the greater metropolitan area around it since he was first elected in 1992. He often wins with more than 60 percent of the vote, and that popular support has empowered him to take bold action. In his 2008 autobiography, he warned that Mexican immigrants feel that "the United States stole the territory that is now California, Arizona and Texas . . . and that massive immigration over the border will speed and guarantee the *reconquista* of these lands, returning them to Mexico." Arpaio titled his book *Joe's Laus: America's Toughest Sheriff Takes On Illegal Immigration, Drugs, and Everything Else That Threatens America*. He felt that the federal government was not doing enough to turn back Mexicans, and he vowed to take matters into his own hands.

To Arpaio, Mexican immigrants were unlike any immigrants

that had come before them. They were often disease-carrying criminals and didn't have the same values as American citizens. "My parents, like all other immigrants exclusive of those from Mexico, held to certain hopes and truths," he wrote in his book. Mexicans were a separate class of people. Most of the Mexicans his department apprehended were, he said, "potential" swine-flu carriers. "They're all dirty," he told *GQ* in 2009.

Indeed, advocates of a more aggressive approach to immigration argued that Mexican immigrants were a double threat. In addition to their covert plan to take over American territory, they also brought a "silent invasion" of diseases. These weren't just people simply looking for jobs. They were parasites to be crushed. One report cited in Buchanan's book warned that sickly immigrants "would endanger children in school and at the movies, anyone standing in range of a rogue cough or sneeze, or patrons of fast-food restaurants whose food might be prepared by an 'invader.'" The report's authors recommended mass deportations.

To kids like Cristian and Lorenzo, getting good grades sometimes seemed like the least of their problems.

ONE WINTER MORNING in 1996, Oscar Vazquez awoke to the smell of burning pine and oak. He was nine years old and got out of bed to see a huge fire in the backyard. A big pot of water was boiling up clouds of steam into the early-morning air of the Sierra Madre Occidental, a rugged mountain range running along the northwestern spine of Mexico. Oscar was thrilled: this meant his father was going to butcher one of the family pigs, a sure sign of an imminent party. Temosachic was a town of about a thousand people and two cars, though Oscar's dad liked to joke that one was always broken. The roads were dirt and the people poor, but they knew how to throw a party. There'd be lots of kids, games, and *carnitas* tacos, his favorite.

Oscar watched as his father led the pig out of its pen. Ramiro Vazquez had a long, furrowed face and a narrow mustache that he shaved below his nose so it ran in a thin line along the top of his lip. He had once been a police officer, but he didn't like the job. The government had given him a broken pistol that would only fire if it was aimed straight up. He eventually quit and now farmed corn. The family also had four cows, three pigs, two horses, a colt, and a mule, so the sacrifice of a pig meant something big was happening. Ramiro tied the pig's hind legs to a fence post, bound the front legs together, and handed his young son the rope.

"*Jala, hijo,*" he told Oscar, ordering him to pull. Oscar hauled as hard as he could. He'd seen animals killed before, but he'd never participated. His dad took out a knife and quickly stabbed the animal. Oscar struggled to hold the pig in place as it thrashed and shook. Blood poured out on the ground. When the animal stopped moving, Oscar slowly released the rope. He wasn't the innocent boy he had been just a few minutes ago.

He asked his father how they were going to butcher the pig. That's when his dad told him that the pig wasn't for *carnitas*. There would be no party, no kids, and no games. They were going to sell the meat to the local butcher to finance Ramiro's journey to the United States. He was leaving the family. The falling price of corn made it hard to pay the bills, particularly when the animals ate so much of the harvest. He had to go *al otro lado*— "to the other side." Oscar was in shock.

Ramiro left a week later, on a Wednesday in 1996. Manuela, Oscar's mother, was nominally in charge, but she quickly fell into a funk. When Oscar left for school in the morning, she sat numbly by the wood-burning stove. When he came home in the afternoon, she was still there, just staring into the fire. Oscar's older brother, Pedro, was seventeen years old but didn't help out much around the house. He had started staying out late with his friends and sleeping late in the morning. Luz, Oscar's sister, was fifteen years old and could do the cooking, but Ramiro's departure effectively made young Oscar the man of the house.

It was difficult. Oscar fed the animals by himself, and when he ran out of hay, he went door-to-door, haggling with his adult neighbors to buy alfalfa with the few pesos the family had. Soon, they had to sell the cows to get by. When it rained, water poured into their home through gaping holes in the rusted roof. Oscar and his sister positioned buckets to catch the downpour.

Ramiro ended up working on a potato farm in Idaho and starting sending one hundred dollars monthly. It was enough to get by on, but Oscar missed his dad. Oscar was in fourth grade and was a standout student. He placed first in the regional academic competition and second in the much-larger state competition. He won a trophy—the first his school had ever received. The teachers showed the trophy at an assembly and even built a makeshift trophy stand out of two battered, old desks. But of course Ramiro wasn't there to see his son's success.

A few weeks after Oscar's eleventh birthday, Ramiro called to say that he had been caught in an immigration raid and was being deported. Oscar didn't know what "deported" meant. He hoped it wasn't painful but was excited if it really meant his dad was coming home. When Ramiro finally made it back to his family in Temosachic, he explained that the immigration agents had streamed into the potato factory; Ramiro had hid behind a bunch of cardboard boxes, but one of his shoes stuck out. The agents had spotted him and sent him back to Mexico.

"It's because I have such big feet," he joked with Oscar.

Oscar didn't understand what his father had done wrong. Was having big feet a crime in the United States? Either way, he was happy that these foreign "agents" had sent his dad back to him. It was nice to have him in the house again. His mother came out of her funk and everything seemed great. His dad had saved a thousand dollars and set about rebuilding their leaking roof with galvanized sheet metal. He also bought Oscar a cool red bicycle.

To Oscar, life returned to normal, but Ramiro wasn't happy. He could make more in an hour at the potato-processing plant in Idaho than he could in an entire day in Temosachic. The financial logic was hard to ignore. After just two weeks at home, he announced that he was returning to the United States. Since there were no pigs to sell this time, he sold his mule to a neighbor. Oscar begged him not to sell the colt, but Ramiro needed the money. He took their two horses to a nearby sausage factory and got good money for them. Oscar was heartbroken and burst into tears at the news.

Ramiro took his son aside and told him another piece of

terrifying news. There would be no monthly payments from the United States. His father was going to save everything he could and use the money to bring the whole family north. He didn't want to be apart anymore, and life was better on the other side of the border.

"It will be a long, long car ride," he told Oscar. He knew Oscar got carsick easily so he wanted his son to understand that this was going to be a challenge. Almost everyone in their small town had traveled to the United States. It was an unspoken rite of passage and it was Oscar's turn.

Early in January 1998, Oscar boarded a bus with his mother. His sister had fallen in love with a local boy and insisted on staying behind. His brother would come later. The bus traveled north through the desert on Highway 17 until it reached Agua Prieta, a dusty border town across from Douglas, Arizona. An older relative met them there and told them to be ready to cross the next day.

Oscar was prepared to meet a grizzled criminal, but the next morning, the cousin introduced them to two nice ladies. The women handed Oscar and his mother green cards—they belonged to people who looked vaguely like them. A few hours later, they drove to the crossing station and a border agent stopped them. Oscar held his card up and smiled. The guy was dressed in green and said a long word that Oscar couldn't understand. Then he waved them through.

They stopped at a Circle K convenience store on the outskirts of Phoenix. It was next to a freeway overpass that amazed Oscar. To an eleven-year-old boy who was accustomed to dirt roads, it looked beautiful. He marveled at the massive conrete on-ramps leading up to it. The bridge itself seemed like an impossibility. It was getting dark, and the smell of oranges was in the air. A house stood beside the store. A sprinkler shot water across the striking green lawn in the front yard. This was clearly a land where anything was possible. Oscar hoped that one day he could live in a house just like it: one with a beautiful lawn and a view of an extraordinary overpass.

Oscar wanted to explore the overpass, but his dad arrived and wrapped him in a huge hug. Ramiro took a good look at his son, then gave him some orange-flavored gummy bears to keep him occupied while Ramiro talked to the ladies in front of the Circle K. The ladies spoke in hushed tones. After a moment, Ramiro handed them an envelope with two thousand dollars in cash and they left.

Oscar's first home in the United States did not resemble the pretty house with the lawn and the view of the overpass. The one-bedroom apartment had peeling paint, a garbage-strewn, dirt front yard, and neighbors who blasted music throughout the night. The apartment was about five hundred square feet, but they had to share it with another family. The Vazquezes took the living room while the other family took the bedroom.

Oscar's parents enrolled him at Isaac Middle School, but like other immigrants before him, he didn't speak English. To him, the teachers sounded as if they were saying one long word after another. He just sat quietly and said "Heer" when his name was called.

Within a few weeks, he was able to get to the right classrooms on time, though it was a short-lived victory. Oscar's sister, Luz, refused to join the family in Phoenix, and their mother's anxiety spiked again. Manuela knew that Luz's uncles and cousins would look after her, but Manuela couldn't bear the separation. She fell into another depression. She stopped eating and grew increasingly despondent. After school one day, Oscar's dad told him that the family's experiment in expatriate living was over. Ramiro would stay in Phoenix, but Oscar and Luz would return to Mexico.

Oscar cried all the way to the border and then got carsick. It wasn't that he wanted to stay in the United States. He just wanted to stay somewhere. But his mother's spirits improved the closer they got to the border.

"That's where Mexico is," his mother pointed out hopefully, indicating a cloud floating far away above the desert. Oscar kept crying. He didn't stop until they crossed back into Agua Prieta and his mother bought him chips. He crammed the snack into his mouth so fast, there was no more room for sobs.

Oscar readapted to his life in the country, but the overpass stayed with him. Now that he knew things like it existed, Temosachic seemed small. He knew he'd have to work hard if he wanted to do more than farm the land. He began helping the town's older ladies carry their groceries and killed their chickens when they wanted chicken soup. In exchange, they gave him a few pesos here and there. He enrolled in the local middle school and, based on his previous academic accomplishments, won a government scholarship. It provided money for his uniform, books, and school supplies.

Eight months after they returned, Manuela's brothers invited the family to Matachic, a town ten miles away. It was October and the town was hosting its annual fall fair. Luz didn't want to go—she offered to clean the house instead. It seemed odd that she'd want to miss the party, but she was an unpredictable teenager. The family shrugged it off and decided to go without her.

Oscar loved the fair, which had a miniature Ferris wheel, bumper cars, and a spinning-teacup ride. His uncles were aces at ring-around-the-bottle and kept winning dried rabbit legs, which they gave to Manuela for good luck. They seemed to think she needed it. After all, the family had just blown two thousand hard-earned dollars on their ill-fated trip to Phoenix.

The rabbit legs worked a strange kind of magic. When they got home, the house was spotless but Luz was gone. Manuela was terrified and asked Pedro to go looking for her. Pedro went to the plaza and decided to play basketball instead. It was an open secret in Temosachic that Luz had eloped with her boyfriend. Even Oscar knew the truth.

"I guess the rabbit legs worked," Oscar told his mother.

"What do you mean?" she snapped. Her daughter was missing; she didn't see the good fortune in that.

"Luz married Luis," Oscar told her plainly. "She's not your problem anymore. Plus, that means an extra plate of food for me."

Manuela started crying. She kept crying until Luz came back a week later with her new husband. Luz was beaming. This is what happened: kids grew up, got married, and started their own lives. Pedro was almost twenty years old now and could also take care of himself. They hadn't had enough money to send him to high school, so he worked odd jobs and supported himself. She only had to worry about Oscar, who was twelve years old now and clearly one of the brightest students in the region.

Manuela was hesitant to return to the United States but felt there would be more opportunity for her youngest son there. Government-run schools charged tuition, and even though the fees were small, they were sometimes hard to meet. In the United States, school was free and she figured the course work would be more demanding. As it was, Oscar finished his schoolwork quickly and then had little to do. Sometimes his teachers gave him special assignments, but those weren't particularly challenging. Though Ramiro had finished only third grade and Manuela had completed sixth, she felt that school was important. It would give Oscar the chance at a better life.

But Oscar didn't want to go back. They had tried it once—it hadn't worked out too well. He loved looking at the freeways and big buildings in Arizona, but he didn't speak the language, they had lived in a crowded apartment, his mom got depressed, and the food tasted like cardboard. He told his mom that he would do fine in Mexico.

She didn't agree and told him to pack a small bag of clothes.

"It doesn't matter how smart you are in Mexico," she told him. "You won't get ahead."

On December 12, 1998, they used what was left of Oscar's scholarship money to buy bus tickets back to Agua Prieta. Manuela initially figured that it would be just as easy to cross as it had been earlier in the year. But the nice ladies who had escorted them across before had been arrested and were now in jail. They would have to hire new "coyotes."

Three of Ramiro's friends had green cards and agreed to coordinate the crossing while Ramiro waited for them in Phoenix. They met Manuela and Oscar in a little plaza in Agua Prieta. Oscar didn't like any of it: he told his mom that he wanted to go back to Temosachic. He wanted to be with his sister and her new husband. He didn't want to cross.

Manuela just said no over and over. Oscar considered throwing a fit and crying, but he was twelve. He wasn't a kid anymore and couldn't resort to that. Still, he was on the verge of screaming.

"If you are strong, I will buy you that on the other side," Manuela said, pointing across the plaza. A little kid was playing with a remote-controlled car. It zipped across the plaza and spun in circles. It was the first time Oscar had seen anything like it. He couldn't figure out how it drove by itself and how the boy controlled it without wires. It seemed like magic and he decided that maybe it might be worth all the trouble of crossing over if that was waiting for him on the other side.

Ramiro's friends had a car, but they didn't want to risk smuggling anybody. Instead, they started driving around town, looking for help. They stopped at a blur of places—an auto-body repair shop, a tire store—and eventually found two guys willing to assist. They claimed to be coyotes—smugglers capable of walking immigrants through the desert and across the border—but they looked more like addicts. One was skinny and had bloodshot eyes. The other was so fat, he looked incapable of walking a long distance. They agreed to guide the mother and child to the United States, but only for an up-front payment.

Ramiro's friends dropped the four off at a spot outside Agua Prieta where the border fence transitioned from an ominous twenty-foot-tall wall of iron to a not-so-intimidating chain-link fence. At the intersection of the two fences, the chain link was busted open to create a six-foot hole. Ramiro's friends pulled away and the coyotes explained the rules: keep up, hide when you see the *migra* trucks, and, no matter what, don't identify them as coyotes if caught by immigration.

The fat guy stared lasciviously at Manuela. Oscar felt a spike of panic. It was open desert and they were out there on their own, just him, his mother, and two questionable guys they'd met an hour ago. Oscar knew he wouldn't be able to fight the men if they attacked his mother, but he could throw a rock hard and his aim was good. As they set off for the edge of the fence, he scanned the ground for suitable rocks. He stayed tense, ready to attack at any moment.

They clambered through the hole in the chain link and trudged north. The sun was about to set and the skinny coyote started jogging. Manuela was wearing shoes with short heels, which made it difficult to walk on the uneven ground. The fat coyote, panting with exertion, stayed close to her. Oscar stuck by his mother's side. He was afraid of getting caught and going to jail. Or worse: his mother could get caught and he'd be left by himself with no idea what to do. He didn't even know where the coyotes were taking them. What if they were getting them lost on purpose, leading them deeper into the desert where no one could help them?

It was dark now and they could barely see the ground. There was a crescent moon and thin clouds. Oscar worried about stepping on a snake or a scorpion. The cold also started to get to him. It had been in the low sixties during the day, but now, with the sun down, the temperature plummeted. He had never been so scared in his life.

After what felt like hours of walking, they arrived at a creek bed. A hundred feet away, an immigration camera rotated on a post, but they moved carefully past it, staying on its blind side until they came up the opposite bank and into an open field with knee-high grass. A dusty road ran through the middle of the field. The skinny coyote pointed to some large brown buildings in the distance. That was their destination, he said. He wanted to pick up the pace, but his chubby friend couldn't catch his breath and begged to go slower.

They were about sixty feet from the road when the skinny coyote hissed for them to get down. A Border Patrol truck was driving up the dirt track right toward them. It had an enclosed cell on the back for captured migrants, but the fat coyote was too exhausted to do anything other than kneel down on one knee. His head popped up above the yellow grass like a jack-in-the-box and he refused to lie down, no matter what anyone said. As the truck went past, they could clearly see the agent looking at them, but the man didn't stop.

"He must have been full," the skinny coyote said. "But he probably called for backup." If they wanted to make it, they needed to run the final distance to the big buildings.

They took off, leaving the fat coyote behind. After what seemed to Oscar like an endless run, they reached the back of one of the buildings. The skinny coyote told them that his job was done. He instructed them to the walk around to the front and go inside. They would be picked up there. Then he disappeared into the darkness.

Manuela and Oscar cautiously moved around the building and stepped into the bright lights shining on the sidewalk. They saw lots of gray and blue shopping carts, and a large, illuminated sign above the entrance said WAL★MART. Oscar had no idea what it was.

They ventured into the store and waited in the garden department. Amid the relative safety of the rakes, shovels, and potted plants, Oscar felt slightly less exposed. He found the moist smell of the potting soil comforting and realized that he was exhausted. "We must have run for hours," he told his mother.

Manuela laughed. "What are you talking about? It's only been twenty minutes since we left Mexico."

Oscar couldn't believe it. "But—"

Manuela shushed him. She was worried that if someone heard them speaking Spanish, it would draw unwanted attention. Oscar was too surprised to say much more anyway. The night seemed endless. Within an hour, Ramiro's friends arrived in the garden department—it was the predesignated pick-up spot. Oscar followed them outside to a brand-new Lincoln that smelled of leather and plastic. Overwhelmed, he fell asleep as soon as he got inside.

He awoke briefly to the smell of hamburgers. Bags of food came through a window of the Lincoln—they were at a drive-through at a Jack in the Box. There was an orange soda and fries. Oscar hadn't eaten for twenty-four hours—all the emotion and travel had made him nauseous. He desperately wanted one of the burgers but wasn't sure he could keep it down. His mother told him to keep resting; she'd keep his burger safe.

They arrived at a house with a big front yard covered in grass. Oscar was surprised. This wasn't like the dump they'd stayed in before. This place looked like the home he'd seen on his first trip—the one he dreamed they'd live in one day.

A family of five owned the home. The Vazquezes would share it, and Oscar remembers a blur of adult and kid faces as his mother led him into a bedroom to sleep. When he woke, he was ravenously hungry and ventured out of the room to look for his hamburger. All he found were empty wrappers. His mother had fallen asleep, and the kids who lived there had devoured his portion. From then on, Oscar was infatuated with Jack in the Box. He calls it "the first restaurant I never ate at."

Oscar returned to Isaac Middle School a year after he'd left it. This time, he started to pick up the English language, but it didn't help him make friends. To many kids, he was an unreliable presence who might just disappear again. So when teachers asked if anybody wanted to participate in a science fair, he decided to raise his hand. If nobody was going to talk to him, he figured he'd entertain himself.

Since he'd grown up in a bean-growing region in Mexico, he chose to study how light and humidity affected the germination of beans. He used a small closet at home to conduct the experiment and meticulously tracked all the variables in a notebook. His teachers were surprised. Just a year earlier, he couldn't speak the language. Now Oscar turned in an in-depth, exhaustively documented report on bean sprouts in English. His report won a two-hundred-dollar prize at the county science fair.

In eighth grade, Oscar was selected to go on a field trip to Arizona State University with a small group of other students. They were shown the sports facilities and science labs. They saw college kids zipping around on bicycles. Everything looked new, big, and magical to Oscar. He didn't say anything, but he started to dream about going to college. He didn't say anything because it seemed like an impossibility. He had no idea what he had to do to get there.

For his parents, Oscar's middle school graduation was a triumph. It signaled that their son was destined to accomplish great things. Oscar was assigned to Carl Hayden and showed up as a freshman with no place in the social pecking order. He didn't want to feel so lost, so he tried out for the football team. It seemed like the thing to do. Unfortunately, he had no idea how to play the game and was summarily cut. He tried playing soccer, but the coach repeatedly benched him for playing rough. Apparently, the style of play he was used to in Mexico wouldn't fly in the United States. It seemed as if nobody wanted him.

During football tryouts, he saw a group of students jogging around the field in desert-camo T-shirts. They moved in perfect formation, as if they were one entity. While the football players ran the bleachers five or six times and collapsed into a heap at the bottom, the camo-clad students ran up and down dozens of times and never seemed to tire. When they got to the bottom, they burst into round after round of push-ups. It was as if they were mocking the oversize, heavily padded ballplayers.

Oscar asked around and found out that those kids belonged to the Reserve Officers' Training Corps. ROTC cadets learned to shoot guns, navigate through the wilderness, and rappel down cliffs. They were issued uniforms and had ranks. To Oscar's thirteen-year-old-eyes, they seemed like action heroes.

He signed up early in his freshman year and was issued his own green uniform. Cadets were required to wear the outfit on Thursdays, and the footballers liked to call them "pickles." Maj. Glenn Goins, the group's instructor, taught his charges to take the abuse stoically and reminded them that the best defense was to make sure they could outrun, outclimb, outshoot, and outthink any aggressor.

Goins and the other cadets welcomed Oscar into the group. The mission of the program was to "inspire young people to become better American citizens," and though most of the cadets were probably not citizens, Goins took an open-minded view. For him, Emma Lazarus's poem at the base of the Statue of Liberty summarized one of the things that made America great:

"GIVE ME YOUR TIRED, YOUR POOR,
YOUR HUDDLED MASSES YEARNING TO BREATHE FREE,
THE WRETCHED REFUSE OF YOUR TEEMING SHORE.
SEND THESE, THE HOMELESS, TEMPEST-TOST TO ME,
I LIFT MY LAMP BESIDE THE GOLDEN DOOR!"

So Goins wasn't about to turn anyone away. The kids were here; he figured the best he could do was teach them about America. No other group had ever welcomed Oscar, so when he put on his green "service uniform," he felt a pride he was unaccustomed to. It was nice to belong somewhere.

His freshman year, ROTC transformed Oscar from a skinny 115-pound kid to a 140-pound dynamo. At the outset, he could barely manage a handful of push-ups, and his pull-ups were laughable. By his junior year, he could fire off seventy-six push-ups in a minute and do set after set of pull-ups. He became the commander of the Adventure Training Team, the most gung ho cadre of cadets. They competed in wilderness races in which they had to haul forty pounds of water up mountains and run with backpacks filled with sand. With Oscar rallying the team, they began to beat ROTC programs from much larger schools.

Unlike other schoolwork, which often felt disconnected from life, ROTC felt real. When Goins explained how to apply a tourniquet, he told the story of a friend who got shot in the leg and was able to keep flying his helicopter because of a self-administered tourniquet. Goins had been an attack helicopter pilot during the Vietnam War and infused his program with a deep sense of morality. At a time when immigrants such as Oscar were referred to as "illegal aliens," Goins taught his students that the Declaration of Independence enshrined all people—not just American citizens—with "unalienable Rights."

"It was the most awesome, coolest thing ever," Oscar says.

Goins felt that everybody should be called to serve the community in some way. That's why he had joined the military, and that's why he continued to teach at Carl Hayden after he had retired from the Army. But he knew that many of his charges couldn't enter the military. Since the Vietnam War, immigrants with green cards had been permitted to enlist. But students who crossed the border illegally were still citizens of their native country and couldn't join.

Oscar didn't know that. He believed he was dutybound to give back to the United States. He was receiving a free education, and his family was able to afford a home that didn't leak. The United States had been good to him and he wanted to show his appreciation. He had only been in the United States for about two years, but he viewed himself as an American now. Particularly after September 11, 2001, he felt that it was his obligation to defend and possibly even die for the country that was his new home.

Soon after 9/11, Oscar sought out Major Goins. "I want to enlist, sir," Oscar said, even though he was only fourteen years old.

Goins hated this part of his job. He figured that about 85 percent of his charges had crossed the U.S. border illegally or overstayed their visas, and while he explicitly told his students that he wasn't recruiting them for the military, many inevitably wanted to join.

"Do you have a green card, son?" Goins asked.

"No, sir," Oscar responded, still bright eyed and innocent.

Goins looked at Oscar with regret. In his nineteen years as an ROTC commander, Goins had never met a finer student than Oscar. He embodied everything the military was looking for: leadership, intelligence, dependability, integrity, tact, selflessness, and perseverance. He was the consummate cadet in all regards except that he wasn't eligible to serve. "Oscar had it all," Goins remembers. "His only drawback was that he wasn't a U.S. citizen."

"You know, there was a time when that was okay," Goins said, thinking back to World War Two and the Vietnam War, when Canadians were allowed to join the U.S. military. "But it's not gonna work anymore. You gotta be a U.S. citizen or a permanent resident."

Oscar felt as if the air had been sucked out of him. He didn't know what to say. He looked at Goins for a moment, but then snapped to attention. This was just an obstacle, nothing more, and it was the mission of a cadet to overcome all obstacles. The bigger the obstacle, the better the opportunity to prove the cadet's mettle.

"Thank you, sir," Oscar said, now recovered from the flash of disappointment. As he walked away, he decided there was only one solution: to become the best cadet the program had ever seen. "Maybe if I'm good enough, something will change," he thought.

When Oscar was a junior, the battalion went to Fort Huachuca, a 110-acre Army base near the Mexican border. Active-duty soldiers ran the teenagers through the camp's obstacle course and gave them puzzles to solve. Oscar gave it everything he had and expected his teammates to follow his example. Running the obstacle course, Oscar hauled people over the walls and picked up their loads if they couldn't carry them. He seemed to be everywhere at once, exhorting his teammates, zipping up ropes and racing under low-slung barbed wire.

He made an impression. Goins promoted Oscar to cadet major, thereby making him the battalion's executive officer. He was now responsible for planning events, coordinating students, and teaching the younger cadets the basics. He also commanded the Adventure Training Team, and under his leadership they became an elite unit within the battalion. It wasn't enough to simply pass the team's physical challenges. Oscar rallied his squad to do training exercises after school and on weekends. Long after the football team had gone home, they jogged around West Phoenix. On Saturdays and Sundays, the team ranged across the mountains surrounding Phoenix, scaling cliffs and fording rivers. When they reached a summit, Oscar led a round of push-ups.

Goins taught a civics class and required his students to study the Preamble to the Constitution. While others simply read it, Oscar memorized it and would recite it to anyone who asked. For him, there was no irony when he said, "We, the People of the United States." It was his reality. He was coming of age in Arizona, and his schooling was preparing him to be a productive member of American society.

At the end of Oscar's junior year, Goins awarded Oscar the JROTC Officer of the Year trophy. Oscar wore his green Army uniform to the ceremony. It bore row after row of ribbons signifying all the medals he had been awarded. The executive officer's whistle and the black Adventure Training cord were slung over his left shoulder. A nameplate over his right pocket read VAZQUEZ. The trophy featured a golden cadet standing at attention, and Oscar held it, beaming, in a photo with Major Goins. It was one of Oscar's proudest moments.

But it wasn't enough. Two other cadets had green cards and enlisted at the end of junior year. Oscar watched as they shipped out for basic training that summer while he stayed home in Phoenix, working at a mattress factory with his father. It was a stark reminder that nothing would change the fact that his mother had taken him across the border at night without a visa.

By the start of his senior year, he realized that he needed to find something else to do with himself. He hadn't worked this hard to end up at a mattress factory like his dad. Ramiro and Manuela had brought the family to Arizona to give Oscar a chance to accomplish more than they had been able to. The problem was, Oscar didn't know what to do now. So when he walked into Fredi Lajvardi's marine science classroom in October 2003, he was ready for new ideas.

FREDI LAJVARDI KNEW how Oscar felt. Like many of his students at Carl Hayden, Fredi arrived in the United States when he was a small child. He was born in Tehran, Iran, in 1965, the son of a successful ophthalmologist and a pediatrician who wanted better career opportunities for their children and themselves. His parents—Reza and Tooran—needed to redo their internships to practice medicine in the United States, so they moved to Cleveland, Ohio, in 1966 when Fredi was just a year old. His brother, Alladin, was born in Cleveland and therefore had automatic U.S. citizenship, something that Fredi wouldn't receive until 1984, when he was nineteen years old.

Reza and Tooran followed jobs to St. Joseph's Hospital in Phoenix in 1969. The family moved into an apartment near the hospital, just north of downtown, and Fredi started elementary school at Candy Cane Elementary. Though his parents spoke Farsi with each other, they spoke English with their children. The emphasis was on assimilating.

But when Fredi turned eight, his parents announced that they were returning to Tehran. Suddenly, Fredi found himself at an international school in Iran. Half the day they spoke English, but the other half, they spoke Farsi. He didn't speak the language and was lost for much of it. Math was particularly challenging since Iranians use a different notation to express numbers. His fellow students made fun of him because, as an eight-year-old, he couldn't even solve 1 + 1. It wasn't that he couldn't do the math; he just couldn't do the math in their language. For the first month, he came home crying every day.

For Fredi, Iran felt like a place he should know but didn't. He was fascinated by the bazaars, which felt wildly exotic, with the strange, pungent smells of carpet and leather shops. The family's duplex in Tehran—with the marble on the walls and a marble exterior façade—seemed equally foreign. He never fully adjusted, and after just a year in Iran, the family decided to return to Phoenix.

For Fredi, Phoenix was home. By the time he was ten years old, the Lajvardis had moved into a forty-six-hundred-square-foot modernist home designed by Paul Yeager, a Frank Lloyd Wright acolyte. Tour buses would ferry architecture buffs past the house while Fredi and his brother waved from the balcony. He felt that the family belonged in Arizona and was respected. After all, both his parents were doctors, and the expectation was that he would go into medicine as well. His future seemed set.

Then revolution erupted in Iran. The American embassy was overrun, and sixty-six Americans were taken hostage. Fredi had just started high school at Camelback High. Kids who had never paid attention to him now identified him as Iranian and began to heckle him. At some restaurants in Phoenix, owners posted signs that read NO IRANIANS. Across the country, Iranians were targeted and attacked.

As the hostage crisis stretched out, the antagonism grew. One day, after cross-country practice during his sophomore year, Fredi headed home on his bike. As he pulled out of the school parking lot, a truck full of teenagers roared up and started yelling, "Damn Iranian!" The driver veered toward Fredi, forcing him into the curb. He flew off the bike and landed on the pavement as the teens poured out of the car and surrounded him. They kicked him until members of the cross-country team started running their way. Fredi's attackers raced off, leaving him in a ball on the ground.

When he got home, he told his parents that he'd fallen off his bike. He was afraid that they'd pull him off the cross-country team if they knew the truth. Part of his coping mechanism was to focus on his running, and he didn't want to lose it. He turned his frustration into speed and went to the state championship every year in the 5K.

His other outlet was building things. In eighth grade, he constructed a hovercraft out of notebook paper and balsa wood. Powered by an electric motor, it could float across a tabletop. He demonstrated it at a regional science fair and caught the attention of Ann Justus, a science teacher at Camelback, who had grown up in Texas.

"Good work," she said in a Texan drawl. "I'm signing you up for my seminar."

It was as if he'd been let into a secret club. It was so secret, he didn't even know what she was talking about. But when he arrived at high school, he saw that he was enrolled in a class called Science Seminar, taught by Justus. He found the classroom and discovered Justus's freewheeling class devoted to building things.

With Justus's encouragement, Fredi's hovercraft quickly became his obsession. Every year, he improved on his initial design, building larger and more ambitious vehicles. Unlike other students, who entered new projects into the yearly science fair, Fredi continued entering his hovercraft, and every year he won first place at the Central Arizona Regional Science and Engineering Fair. What began as something the size of a toaster grew into a six-hundred-pound, sit-on-top, gasoline-powered hovercraft by 1983, his senior year. It ran off of a repurposed sixty-horsepower snowmobile engine and could reach speeds of twenty-five miles per hour.

The local news heard of the mechanical wunderkind at Camelback and dispatched Jerry Foster, a pioneering helicopter news reporter, to cover the story. Foster landed his Bell 206 JetRanger copter on the Camelback football field, making Fredi an instant celebrity on campus. Even though his hovercraft looked like a partially deflated orange life raft with a large white fan mounted at the front, it worked. Fredi had painted the words DOS EQUIS on the side, and he rode on the back wearing oversize, clear plastic laboratory glasses. "I probably could have had three girlfriends that day if I was focused on that," he says. In reality, he looked like a supergeek and had no girlfriend.

His parents didn't think much of his "toy." To them, it was just a distraction from schoolwork. Building useless conveyances wasn't going to get him ahead in life, they argued. Getting a medical degree would.

When he started college at Arizona State University, he began the premed track but found himself drawn back to Justus's Science Seminar at Camelback High. He would drop in to visit his former teacher after class and help younger students develop their projects. It was much more interesting than the dry lectures he attended and the seemingly pointless memorization required.

At Camelback, Justus watched him working with the students and was impressed. When it came to helping kids build things, he was brimming with enthusiasm and had a natural ability to get the kids excited too. If a kid wanted to figure out if the size of a fish tank affected fish growth, Fredi was ready to help track down a bunch of fish tanks. Interested in holograms? Fredi had suggestions about laser wavelengths. A solar-powered barbecue? Fredi thought it was a great idea.

During his freshman year at ASU, Justus took him aside on one of his visits to her classroom. "You know you're just wasting your time with this premed stuff," she told him. "You're meant to be a teacher."

Fredi laughed. It seemed like a ridiculous suggestion. He was going into sports medicine. He'd combine his interest in running with what his parents expected of him. It'd be great.

But by his sophomore year, he just couldn't focus anymore on the college science classes. They felt entirely detached from the real world. He decided that architecture might be more hands-on so he dropped out of the premed track. To get into the undergraduate architecture program, students had to complete an array of prerequisite courses and then apply. For the next two years, Fredi worked through the course work and then sent in his application. He wasn't a straight-A student but figured his enthusiasm would tip the balance. After all, architecture seemed like the perfect fit for him: it was a mix of construction and science.

He was blindsided when his application was rejected. The school of architecture wasn't interested in him. The rejection was doubly painful because Ali, his younger brother, was an academic ace who had just graduated from Camelback tied for valedictorian. Ali was bound for the premed track at the University of California at San Diego and would go on to get his medical degree at Johns Hopkins, eventually specializing in vascular and interventional radiology. He seemed to be fulfilling the family's expectations.

Fredi, on the other hand, was spending his free time hanging out at Justus's workshop with teenagers who were building strange and often useless contraptions. His mother encouraged him to spend more time studying instead; that might help him do better and get back on some kind of respectable track. Fredi knew he had to do something; he just didn't know what.

Justus continued to remind Fredi that there was a simple, obvious answer: he should be a teacher. But Fredi had a slew of reasons why it didn't make sense.

"People don't respect teachers," he added.

"Who cares what other people think?" she fired back. "You're happy when you're here, aren't you?"

Fredi didn't want to concede the point. "No offense, but I've seen the cars teachers drive. They're worse than the students'."

"Who cares what car you drive?"

"Teachers make no money," he said, almost begging her to admit that it wasn't a good career choice.

"Money's not everything."

Fredi ran out of arguments.

Justus just stared at him until he squirmed under her glare. "You're making a difference in people's lives."

"I don't want to be a teacher," he said.

"Quit messing around," she ordered. "You're already a teacher."

Fredi returned to ASU and started taking education courses. He discovered that most of his course work would count toward a degree in secondary education with a science focus. Compared to the other class work he had done, the education courses felt natural and easy. He was assigned to student-teach at Camelback, and when he showed up for his first staff meeting, Justus made an announcement: "He finally listened to me."

Everybody clapped.

The reaction at home was less supportive. Fredi's first full-time teaching job was at Carl Hayden, where he replicated Justus's Science Seminar. His energy caught the attention of the Phoenix Jaycees, a charitable organization of businessmen, who named Fredi the city's Most Innovative Teacher in 1988. When he took the trophy home to show his mother, she didn't show much interest.

"When are you going to go get a real degree?" she asked.

Fredi couldn't believe it. Growing up, his mother had always told him to be the best at whatever he did. Now he'd proven that he was a great teacher, but it wasn't good enough.

"You're breaking your father's heart being a teacher," his mother said.

Fredi felt as if he'd been punched in the stomach. He turned and walked out.

In 1996, Fredi married Pam Nuñez, the school psychologist

at Carl Hayden. Far from giving up on teaching, he was putting down roots. He coached cross-country and started an electric-car racing program. His students built vehicles that could rocket up to a hundred miles per hour. Still, the tension with his parents remained.

In 1997, Pam and Fredi had their first child, a boy they named Bijan. Alex, another boy, was born in 1999. They bought a nice house in Gilbert, a town in East Phoenix, and Pam took time off to raise the children. Toward the end of 2001, she was considering going back to work when it became clear that something was different about Alex. At age two, he began talking in full sentences, but then, over a period of three months, he stopped speaking.

"It was like a light switch turned off," Fredi says.

Alex was diagnosed with pronounced autism. He moved in repetitive patterns, burst into angry frustration for unclear reasons, and couldn't engage in normal social interactions. It was as if he were living in a parallel universe. At the same time, Bijan, the older boy, was struggling with social settings. Loud noises bothered him; if a group of kids broke into laughter, Bijan cringed. Later, he would explain that the noise was "painful." By 2002, he was diagnosed with Asperger's syndrome, a less severe form of autism that made socializing difficult but also provided unique insights into the world.

Soon after the diagnosis, Fredi's parents moved out of state. The relationship had been strained for years, but now it worsened. Fredi was in the midst of the most challenging experiences of his life and ended up facing it without their support. His parents settled in Las Vegas, where Ali practiced medicine. They called infrequently and, eventually, stopped communicating altogether. Fredi felt as if he never measured up to their expectations.

It hurt, but he had other things to focus on. He had two young kids, both of whom needed a great deal of attention. In 2002, when Cristian and Lorenzo were freshmen, Fredi scaled back his extracurricular activities. He apologized to the students he coached on the cross-country team and shut down his after-school electric-car program. He wasn't going to have time for all that anymore.

That's when Cristian Arcega walked into his room wanting to build robots. Soon after that, Oscar Vazquez and Lorenzo Santillan arrived, desperate for new ways to define themselves.

IN 1989, inventor Dean Kamen came to work early on a rainy Saturday morning in Manchester, New Hampshire. He was thirty-eight, hefted a briefcase, and wore a denim button-up and jeans—denim on denim was his daily uniform. He was pleased to see that the parking lot was full. He assumed it meant that his staff of engineers was hard at work on a weekend day. But when he got to his office building, he didn't see engineers. He saw kids everywhere.

In his twenties, Kamen had invented a self-regulating syringe that was safer and more reliable than a human-administered shot. When he turned thirty, he sold his company to a large health-care firm, netting himself a sizable fortune. He used some of the money to buy an old textile mill on the bank of the Merrimack River in Manchester and converted the top two floors into a private research-and-development laboratory. He kept the bottom floor clear and spent about three hundred thousand dollars constructing a science museum. He didn't charge admission and built a lot of the exhibits himself. It was his way of giving back to the community, and he was pleasantly surprised that the space had attracted so many kids, particularly on a weekend. It seemed as though his new museum was turning into a hit.

Rather than go immediately up to his office, Kamen wandered through the museum. Children were bouncing in his antigravity machine, blowing giant bubbles at the bubble display, and making their hair stand on end at the electrostatic machine. He strolled past the Bernoulli Blower and watched kids marvel at the way the ball just floated in place above the fan. There was a sense of chaos and excitement. The kids were clearly having fun.

"I was feeling real good," Kamen recalls. "I didn't realize that I was about to have a transformative experience that would ruin my nights and weekends for the next twenty-three years."

Kamen stopped a kid wearing a Boston Celtics jersey and asked if there were other science experiments the kid would like to see. It was as if Willy Wonka had asked what kind of candy bar to make next, but the kid just shrugged and said, "I don't know."

"Well, what do you think's really cool in technology?" Kamen persisted.

"I don't know."

Kamen thought he'd try a different angle. "Do you know any famous scientists or inventors?" he asked, thinking an exhibit could be built around a personality. The kid shook his head.

Kamen wanted to forget about it and get to work, but he decided to try again with another kid. He got the same response: the next boy didn't know any inventors either. Kamen asked a dozen kids if they could name any living engineer, scientist, or inventor, and none of them came up with anything. Frustrated, he decided to ask the parents; they couldn't think of any.

"This isn't mud wrestling," Kamen thought to himself. "This is a science center, so these are already a self-selecting group of the crème de la crème."

Finally, one dad had a burst of inspiration: "Einstein! But I think he's dead."

Kamen walked out frustrated and annoyed. "Who am I kidding?" he thought. He was subsidizing the wealthy kids one at a time, reaching a population that probably didn't need the extra help anyway. And the idea didn't scale. "In the grand scheme of things, this will probably have no measurable impact on the world," he concluded.

By the time he got up to his office on the second floor, he'd decided that kids didn't need more access to knowledge. There were plenty of books, and the information age was about to erupt: there was already an overwhelming supply of knowledge. He realized that kids just weren't that interested in science and technology, certainly in comparison to other things. Their heroes were mostly sports stars, and Kamen fumed that kids were pursuing sports careers that would never pan out. "They're thinking that if they work hard bouncing a ball for the next ten years, they'll be the next great basketball player," he groused.

Kamen had a bolt of inspiration: "I've got to create something that doesn't compete with other science centers; it's got to compete with the World Series and the Super Bowl. I've got to find a way to make science and technology cool."

He decided to start a robot contest. He wanted it to be a finite experience, like a sports season, with a series of events leading up to a championship. There had to be superstars, so he recruited mentors from Apple, IBM, and eventually Google. The goal was to show kids what engineers looked like: young men and women of all backgrounds who made good money, drove nice cars, and were as interesting as the people who bounced balls for a living.

The initial contest was held in February 1992 at Memorial High School in Manchester. The twenty-eight teams were composed of high schoolers predominantly from the Northeast. Kamen paired teams up with engineers from big-league companies such as ATT, Boeing, Alcoa, GE, IBM, and Xerox. He wasn't looking for financial support: he asked the professionals to donate their nights and weekends during the six weeks leading up to the event. Their job was to mentor teens and show them what it meant to think like an engineer.

The event was a lot of fun. Kamen constructed a twelve-foot-by-twelve-foot field and sprinkled it with tennis balls. Three teams faced off against three others, and whichever alliance collected the most balls moved on to the next round. He called the competition FIRST, which stands for For Inspiration and Recognition of Science and Technology. The emphasis was on cooperation and ingenuity, and it proved to be a combustible mix. Every year, the FIRST competition grew, spreading across the country. By 2001, the 13 regional competitions had approximately 25,000 teens competing on 520 teams.

Fredi saw a flyer about FIRST in 1999 and thought it sounded like a good way to get kids involved in something hands-on. But when he decided to start a small team at Carl Hayden in 2000, he quickly realized he couldn't do it alone. The robots needed to be programmed, and Fredi had never studied computer science. He liked designing things and then building them with hammers and saws. The nuance of coding didn't interest him. Plus, by 2001, his family life was forcing him to cut back on his extracurricular activities. He was going to need some help.

ALLAN CAMERON was a mischievous kid. In the fifties, when his parents refused to let him have sleepovers with neighborhood friends, he ran wires between their houses in San Francisco and connected telephones so they could talk into the wee hours on their own private network. Now, as an adult living in Chandler, he'd erected a thirty-foot-tall radio antenna in his backyard so that he could talk to ham-radio operators around the world. (He liked to call the antenna the "communication center of the Western Hemisphere"; his wife, Debbie, calls it "a great big pole outside my bedroom window.") To his colleagues at Carl Hayden, where he was a computer science teacher, he sometimes seemed like a big kid.

Because he had never lost touch with his youth, Allan understood how his students felt. When he was a kid, he hated homework, viewed it as a waste of time, and never did it. So, as a teacher, he rarely assigned homework. It was more important to have real experiences of the world. In the nineties, when the Internet was still in its infancy, he carted in his ham equipment and taught kids how to connect with people in Russia and Japan and astronauts in orbit.

At fifty-five, Allan's bushy beard had already gone gray, but his hair was still brown and usually tousled. He had the shaggy appearance of a hippie, a look he cultivated after serving in the Navy during the Vietnam War. At the time, he decided he no longer wanted to be part of what he viewed as the military-industrial complex and instead started working as an assistant for a philosophy professor at Mesa Community College in Arizona. When the professor suggested that he become a teacher, Allan was doubtful he'd get hired. With his beard and long hair, he looked like Sasquatch. He was also worried that his legal record might disqualify him. In the early seventies, while camping with friends on the Salt River east of Phoenix, two park rangers appeared. They searched his van, found marijuana, and charged him with possession of an illicit substance. Allan thought the arrest might pop up on a background check.

"If a perfect record were a prerequisite, there'd only be about two teachers in all of the state of Arizona," his professor said.

Allan decided to give it a try. He finished a degree in elementary education and happily landed a job at Vista del Camino in South Scottsdale. It was not a plum assignment. Despite being on the East Side of Phoenix, South Scottsdale was a pocket of poverty in the midst of an otherwise wealthy area. The school had a large population of Yaqui Indians and Hispanic kids. Allan was excited to get started, but an administrator warned him that it wouldn't be easy. "It's not the Scottsdale you think of," he said. He acted as if Allan were meat being thrown to the wolves.

The fifth graders he was meant to teach had run off their original teacher. They were unruly and disrespectful. At the beginning of the year, the class had about thirty students, but now only the twelve worst were left. Any parent who was paying attention had pulled their child out of the class. The remaining students had no expectation of learning. Everybody, it seemed, had given up on them.

Allan started with threats. He didn't really know much about teaching, so he was winging it. A kid threw a chair—Allan yelled and sent him to the principal. The next day, the kid paid even less attention and continued to act out. Allan yelled more and tried calling parents, who seemed disengaged. The class got rowdier. Clearly, intimidation didn't work. In fact, it seemed to have the opposite effect.

Allan pulled one of the most unruly kids aside and tried a

different tactic. He explained the importance of education and how it would help the kid throughout his life. The kid was unimpressed. "We're the worst kids in the school," he said with a touch of pride. "We don't care."

For Allan, it was a moment that would affect him and the students he taught for years to come. He realized that the kids were acting out to maintain their bad reputation. It might have been a pejorative label, but it was all they had. "At least they're the best at something," he thought.

The next day, Allan came into class with a challenge: "Okay, look, everyone thinks you guys are a bunch of jerks. Let's change it around. Let's absolutely make you guys the best in the school."

That got their attention, but not much more. Allan explained that he was in the Navy during Vietnam, and he offered to teach them what he knew about war. He had no intention of teaching them to fight, but he knew it would appeal to them.

"What do we gotta do?" one of the kids asked suspiciously.

"We're gonna start marching."

Allan managed to get them lined up, then designated a couple of kids as "sergeants" tasked with keeping the others in line. After teaching them the basic steps, Allan deliberately stayed back, giving the kids room to assert themselves. The class got into it and began marching around the school in perfect lockstep during lunch and recess. Their discipline established a new reputation for them at the school: the kids now wanted to prove that they could be more disciplined than anyone else. They were still tough, but now in a more focused, driven way. Allan boiled it down to a straightforward observation: "Everybody's got to be a hero somehow with something."

In 1982, Allan started a Ph.D. in elementary education, but did about half his course work in the computer science department. He was four years into the program when he heard about Carl Hayden. It was 1986 and the high school had just been designated a computer science magnet school in the district's effort to attract white students. The school was desperate for computer science teachers willing to work "across valley." Allan had been flirting with the idea of teaching at the college level but drove over to West Phoenix to take a look.

Allan rarely went to West Phoenix. Sometimes, when he was driving down the 10 freeway and needed gas, he'd pull off on Thirty-Fifth or Forty-Third. But, beyond that, he'd had little exposure to the neighborhood. At first, he balked at the idea of working in the ghetto. His Ph.D. would open up new possibilities: he could find lucrative work as an educational consultant, land a prestigious professorship, or publish books. Teaching computer science to impoverished students in West Phoenix wasn't going to make him rich—far from it—nor would it bring him much acclaim.

But after teaching some classes at Carl Hayden as a substitute, Allan couldn't stop thinking about the school. He worried that collegiate academia would be filled with meaningless bureaucracy and annoying oversight. He'd be pressured to publish incessantly to get tenure. At Carl Hayden, he'd be teaching programming, a subject no one else knew anything about, so he somewhat naively assumed that it would be hard for anybody to boss him around. He also figured that he'd be free to create his own curriculum. And fundamentally, he was pretty sure the kids in West Phoenix needed his help more than students already in college.

In 1987, he accepted a full-time teaching job at Carl Hayden, and by the time he completed his Ph.D. in 1990, he had no intention of leaving. He was having too much fun. He started programming and ham-radio clubs in the nineties, then signed on to start a robotics team with Fredi in 2000. He didn't regret the decision not to teach at the college level. He didn't speak Spanish or know much about Mexico or Central America. But most of the kids he met at Carl Hayden were hungry to learn and willing to work hard. After a couple of years, he couldn't imagine leaving them.

THE CARL HAYDEN robotics team got off to a slow start. In 2001 and 2002, only a handful of kids signed up. In 2003, they entered the Arizona regionals and placed thirty-first out of thirty-seven. The poor showing wasn't surprising. They were a brand-new team and didn't know what they were doing. Plus, Fredi had had to scale back his commitment to stay home with Pam and the kids. Not many students knew about the group, and Fredi didn't have a lot of time to talk it up.

But the kids who did show up were thrilled to be a part of the team. Michael Hanck, a video-game-obsessed freshman, had taken one of Fredi's marine science classes and joined the team that same year. Hanck had gone to middle school with Cristian and knew that the diminutive Mexican kid loved machines. He suggested Cristian talk to Fredi.

During a free period, Cristian loped up the stairs of the 200 building and stepped into Fredi's classroom. Partially assembled robots were lying around: a chassis here, a circuit board there. It was May—school was almost over—and the team had already competed in that year's FIRST competition. But Fredi had a video of the event and played it for Cristian. It looked amazing, but it was all over now. The robot had already been disassembled. There didn't seem to be anything to do. He'd have to wait another year. Plus, Fredi seemed tired and was ready to go home.

Fredi was in fact exhausted. Raising an autistic son had turned his life upside down, emotionally and financially. Pam never went back to work, so they had to make do with one income. It was hard to summon the energy to engage with students all day, let alone get through his nearly hour-long commute. But he didn't want to disappoint the quiet, thoughtful kid standing in front of him.

"We're gonna build a trebuchet next," Fredi pointed out. "You could help us out."

"What's a treb-ooo-shay?"

"It's a medieval, gravity-operated catapult," Fredi said, as if it were the most obvious thing in the world. "We're going to fire pumpkins out of it at Halloween."

"That sounds awesome." It was the first time Cristian had encountered something at school that sounded exciting. But he was also cautious. He was accustomed to being let down, so he tried not to get too excited.

It was hard to restrain himself. Cristian started using his free time to hang around the marine science lab. Fredi showed him a video of former students converting a Pontiac Fiero into an electric car. The students challenged the local police to a race at a training track and beat the cop car. They had also built an electric vehicle that looked like a Formula 1 race car. "This is cool," Cristian thought to himself.

Fredi was impressed by Cristian's smarts. The kid had the second-highest GPA in his grade, and when Fredi needed to install a batch of new computers, Cristian volunteered to set up a LAN—a local area network—so that the computers could work together. Book smarts were good, but Fredi appreciated Cristian's ability to assemble something up on the fly.

Cristian started to see another kid hanging around the lab. Lorenzo had been assigned to take Introduction to Marine Science and cycled through the room four times a week for class. To Cristian, he was just another loudmouth—the type of guy who cracked jokes in class and caused useless distractions. Cristian was quick to refer to people like that as "idiots."

But Fredi saw something else in Lorenzo. He saw an unusual

kid who was lost and looking for a way to define himself. After the xylophone debacle in band, Lorenzo was adrift. His cousins had started a gang called WBP—for Wet Back Pride. They taught Lorenzo their hand signs and let him hang out with them. It was a way of belonging to something, but he didn't want to get in trouble. He wasn't that tough.

Fredi noticed that Lorenzo lingered after class. The mullet-haired kid would noodle around the fish tanks and listen to Fredi talk about building things. What seemed to really capture his attention were all the tools in the closet across the hallway. There were more tools in there than Hugo had, and students were allowed to use them. But Lorenzo was accustomed to hanging back, so he just watched as Fredi fed the fish and scrubbed the tanks over lunch.

One day, Fredi offered him the scrubber, motioning toward the tanks. "You want to learn how to do this?"

Lorenzo laughed nervously. "Uh, sure." He'd never had much responsibility. Lorenzo felt his father didn't have any respect for him, Hugo wouldn't let him use the tools in the driveway, and the kids around school mocked him for his strange looks. Now a teacher was entrusting him with the lives of a handful of fish. To most people, it might not seem like a lot, but to Lorenzo it was unprecedented.

Fredi explained how much food to put in each tank and how to clean algae off the aquarium walls. Looking after the tanks quickly became part of Lorenzo's routine. When it was time to do a thorough cleaning, he came in on a Saturday to help Fredi partially drain the tanks. It was smelly work; some kids complained. But Lorenzo had dealt with worse. He sometimes fished for tilapia in concrete canals that reeked of sewage. (It made for an inexpensive meal.) So, when Fredi asked for his help, he enthusiastically said yes. He was honored to be asked.

After the tanks had been scrubbed, Fredi invited Lorenzo to McDonald's. Lorenzo didn't know exactly what to say. Nobody had taken him to a restaurant before, not even for fast food. His family ate beans most days; there was no extra money to spend on luxuries such as a meal out. Fredi didn't know any of this. He just hustled Lorenzo into his Chevy Silverado truck and drove them over to Thirty-Fifth and Van Buren.

At the McDonald's, Lorenzo stood nervously in line beside Fredi. He didn't know what to order and was worried that he'd get something that was too expensive.

"What do you want?" Fredi asked.

"You go first."

Fredi ordered a Big Mac with fries.

"I'll have that too," Lorenzo chimed in.

When they sat down, Fredi started telling Lorenzo about robotics. He explained that students on the team got to use all the tools in the robotics closet, from the hacksaws to the drills. It was a chance to learn computer programming and mechanical engineering, both of which were skills that could help get him into college. It was also fun. The trebuchet was a great example: their goal was to build a catapult that could hurl a pumpkin more than a hundred feet.

Fredi didn't need to say all that: he had Lorenzo at hacksaws and drills.

ONE BEAUTIFUL SUNDAY during the summer of 2002, a group of Phoenix high school students from Wilson Charter High School went to visit Niagara Falls. Wilson was a small school of 370 kids that was focused on giving low-income and minority students expanded opportunities. Teachers—including Julia Reaney—had organized this trip to Buffalo, New York, for the students to compete in a solar-powered boat race, and they were using their spare time to do some sightseeing. It was seventy-five degrees and clear—a perfect day to watch 757,500 gallons of water a second drop off a cliff. For kids from the desert, it was an astonishing sight.

Over the school year, the kids from Wilson High had worked hard to convert a small rowboat into a solar-powered dinghy. Their little boat had won a regional competition, earning them a place at Solar Splash, the "World Championship of Intercollegiate Solar Boating." The event was sponsored by the Institute of Electrical and Electronics Engineers, and the Wilson kids were thrilled to be there. It was a chance to learn a lot and see new places. One boy described it as a "once-in-a-lifetime opportunity."

The falls were top on the list of places to see. They had Sunday off, so they drove to the visitors' center and looked out over the roar and tumble of water. It was impressive, but they were right beside the falls. To get a view of the whole thing, they'd have to cross the Rainbow Bridge to the Canadian side. Reaney knew that some of her students were from Mexico—roughly 95 percent of the student population was Hispanic—and many likely lived in the United States illegally. She didn't want to take any undue risks, so she walked across the large parking lot that separated the visitors' center from the Port of Entry building.

Inside, she found an immigration agent and asked if kids with U.S. school IDs would be allowed to cross. She assumed that if it wasn't allowed, she'd simply stroll back to the visitors' center, tell the kids to pack up, and drive back to the competition. But the immigration agent's interest was piqued. He wanted to know where the kids were from and what their backgrounds were.

When the agent heard that the kids were waiting at the visitors' center, he marched across the parking lot and began quizzing them. He asked where they were born and wanted proof of U.S. citizenship. Four of the kids had been brought across the U.S.-Mexican border as children, and though they'd grown up in Phoenix, they were living in the country illegally. It didn't matter that they were some of the top students at their high school, nor that they had come here to participate in an engineering competition. The agent decided to detain them. They were led to a holding area inside one of the immigration buildings, and over a nine-hour stretch, a series of agents interrogated them. When one kid admitted that he was born in Mexico, an agent demanded to know where he had crossed the border.

"Man, I was like two," the teen said. "I have no idea."

"What are you guys doing coming to Niagara Falls?" another agent said. "You really stick out here."

Immigration agents phoned Jane Juliano, the principal of Wilson Charter High School, and asked her to fax birth certificates for the four detained students. According to Juliano, the agents wanted to make a point.

"Don't send your illegals to New York," one agent told her over the phone.

The agents began proceedings to deport the four students to Mexico. The legal wrangling dragged on in federal court for three years before a judge ruled that the students had unfairly been targeted based on their Hispanic appearance. The Justice Department appealed, but a federal immigration appeals board threw the case out and the four were allowed to stay in the United States.

Nonetheless, the threat was clear: students who were living in the country illegally could be sought out and detained. A Border Patrol agent could find these kids anywhere and send them to a country they barely knew. Attempts to excel might be met with harsh punishment. Even a seemingly harmless summer science competition bore life-altering risks.

WHEN THE 2003-2004 school year started, Lorenzo and Cristian both signed up for the 7:00 a.m. robotics club class. Together with Michael Hanck, the newly minted sophomores began constructing a massive catapult. The teenage boys were given free access to power tools for the first time in their lives. So rather than design a modest device that could easily be transported, Hanck drew up a schematic for a five-hundred-pound giant that stood fifteen feet tall and rolled on four-foot-diameter wooden wheels. Cristian and Lorenzo agreed it was awesome. If it was a catapult, it needed to look appropriately medieval. Hanck dubbed it the MOAT, aka the Mother of All Trebuchets. As the boys enthusiastically began to assemble their enormous hurling contraption, Fredi worried that the project might take a detour into a fantasy world. The boys needed some leadership.

Fredi had an ideal candidate. Oscar Vazquez was in Fredi's senior Marine Science Seminar and was a standout cadet in the ROTC program. Though Oscar had the hoo-ha spirit, he clearly wasn't going to be able to make a career in the Army. He enrolled in Fredi's class to experiment with new opportunities and approached the seminar with typical gusto. He didn't want to just take the class, he wanted to push himself and everyone around him to do something amazing.

So when Fredi mentioned that a bunch of the kids were building a catapult in the science-and-technology club, Oscar listened closely. He liked building things and was adept with power tools after countless weekends working with his father at the mattress factory. But more important, he was looking for a new team to lead. He agreed to check it out.

What Oscar saw impressed him. Hanck's trebuchet design featured a wooden tower that supported a bench-press bar fifteen feet off the ground. The bar was loaded with 120 pounds, and when released, it whipped a twelve-foot-long two-by-four through a 180-degree arc, hurling whatever was on the end into the distance.

It looked cool, but Oscar could see a fundamental problem. Because the arm extended twelve feet, the leverage required to pull the 120-pound weight back into firing position was substantial. At 120 pounds, Cristian could dangle off the arm and the structure would barely budge. This bunch of skinny nerds had built a catapult so big, it would be difficult to fire.

Oscar was well suited to solve the problem. As the commander of the Adventure Training Team, he was accustomed to scaling rock walls and dangling from ropes. He regularly ordered his ROTC squad to crawl on each other's back to form a pyramid. This would be no different. Oscar grappled up a rope to the top of the trebuchet arm, adding some initial downward motion. Then, with Cristian, Lorenzo, Hanck, and others in the club pulling down, the group's combined weight was enough to lower the bench-press bar into the firing position.

The big unveiling of the trebuchet was scheduled for October 2003 at Mother Nature's Farm in Gilbert, Arizona. The local pumpkin patch hosted an annual pumpkin-hurling contest; cash prizes and bragging rights were at stake. Lorenzo was excited. He had never hung out with seniors, let alone someone as serious and focused as Oscar. He was also impressed by Cristian's smarts, and the fact that they had built something twice as tall as any of them. The day before the contest, Fredi told the group that they would leave at six the next morning. The pumpkin patch was a half-hour drive, and they needed time to assemble the trebuchet when they got there. Lorenzo couldn't wait to see it in action.

But the next morning, Lorenzo slept late and woke up a few minutes before six. He lived ten minutes from the school and leapt on his twenty-speed bike. Unfortunately, only two gears worked, and they were the high gears. He jumped on and strained to get going, but the gearing was tough. He could barely move the bike at first. Once he got going, he flew down the predawn streets, pedaling wildly.

He was within a block of campus when the school van flew past him and turned onto the freeway on-ramp. The van was pulling the trebuchet on a trailer; Lorenzo watched as it accelerated onto the interstate and disappeared down the ramp. He had spun himself into exhaustion and couldn't even yell. He was two minutes late. He was furious with himself and his lack of discipline.

Out at the pumpkin field, the guys didn't miss Lorenzo. Cristian didn't have a lot of respect for him to begin with, and his absence only reinforced Cristian's initial impression. Nor was Oscar impressed with someone who couldn't wake up on time. That was drilled into every cadet: there's no excuse for being late. Lorenzo had a long way to go to earn the group's trust.

The pumpkin-chucking event began, and Oscar, Cristian, and Hanck struggled to arm the trebuchet. Cristian was wearing black shorts that hung below his knees with white socks pulled up his calves. He sported a white, too-big T-shirt and the wisp of a mustache. He looked like a nerdy gangster. Oscar wore a tank top and a crew cut and muscled his way up the rope to pull the catapult's arm down. Hanck pulled from the midpoint, while Cristian dangled off the rope at the bottom. It took all three of them to get the arm into position. When they fired it, the device made a satisfying *whoosh* and flung the pumpkin about one hundred feet.

By adding more weight, the kids were able to increase the "rate-of-hurl," inching up to a hundred and fifty feet. That placed them in second, behind a school from a relatively affluent part of

East Phoenix. In an effort to overtake their competitors, they added more and more weight to the contraption. Finally, the trebuchet arm snapped in half. Carl Hayden had to content themselves with second place, but everybody agreed it had been a lot of fun. The only problem had been that it was difficult to handle such a large, cumbersome machine. They realized that it would be helpful to have somebody a little bigger on the team.

LUIS ARANDA STARTED out as a perfectly normal-size six-pound baby. Maria Garcia Aranda, his mother, thought he looked like a beautiful little doll and showed him off to her friends. The family lived in a shack in the Mexican city of Cuernavaca with intermittent running water and power. Looking back, nobody could quite pinpoint why Luis had turned into a giant. Maybe it was toxins in all the nopals and loquats he ate, or something in the water they siphoned off a cistern, but he started to grow and grow. Both his parents were five feet five inches, but by kindergarten, Luis was one of the tallest and heaviest youngsters in the neighborhood.

Maria Garcia worked as a housecleaner for a Japanese woman. Many days, Maria Garcia would bring Luis to work, and the Japanese woman took a liking to the stout little boy. He was big without exactly being fat. In many ways, he had the solidity and presence of a sumo wrestler. The lady watched as Luis lumbered around the property and played in the dirt. One day, when Luis told his mother that he loved her, the Japanese lady got emotional. "I remember when my children used to say that to me," she said.

The Japanese woman knew that the Aranda family was struggling. Luis's father, Pedro, worked as a construction laborer but left to find work in the United States as a farmworker. Maria Garcia had completed only second grade and got married when she was fourteen. Now she was pregnant with another child. There seemed to be a win-win solution: friends of the Japanese woman approached Maria Garcia and suggested she put Luis up for adoption. The Japanese lady would take good care of him. He'd be well fed, well clothed, and maybe even get to visit Japan.

But Maria Garcia couldn't part with her son, even if that meant he'd have limited opportunities. Nonetheless, the conversation forced her to consider what she could do to give Luis a better life. Taking him to the United States felt like the only real option.

On Sunday, July 21, 1991, Maria Garcia packed a small bag and took Luis by the hand. "We're going somewhere else," she said. Together with his grandfather, an aunt, and two cousins, the family set off for Nogales by bus. They walked through a hole in a chain-link fence on the border and took a taxi to Phoenix, where Pedro had found work as a butcher. Eventually, Pedro obtained permanent residency in the United States and was able to get green cards for Maria Garcia and Luis as well. That meant Luis was one of the lucky kids who didn't have to live in fear of deportation.

As Luis grew up in Phoenix, he expanded more rapidly. By fourteen, he was taller than his parents, and by sixteen, he was 205 pounds and six feet tall, a full seven inches taller than either of his parents. He was a quiet kid, but it wasn't a brooding or sullen quiet. He seemed to look out on the world from on high with subtle bemusement, as if everything smaller people did was slightly funny.

He wasn't particularly interested in school—reading tended to make him fall asleep—but he knew that his parents had made sacrifices to bring him to the United States, and he didn't want to let them down. He dutifully went to school, but the family had also grown and there were a lot of mouths to feed. Maria Garcia gave birth to David in 1991, Joselin in 1996, and Miguel in 2000. In middle school, Luis started washing dishes at Amici's, an Italian restaurant. From age eleven onward, he'd get out of school at 3:00 and work at the restaurant from 4:00 to 10:00 p.m.

Compared to school, the kitchen fascinated Luis. Luis silently watched the chefs churn out dishes he'd never seen or heard of: fettuccine Alfredo, chicken lasagna, and shrimp scampi. At home, Luis started watching cooking shows on TV and was entranced by the way Julia Child cooked roast turkey. He asked his mom to make a dinner that way and she did her best. She bought a turkey, boiled it in broth, and served it with a thick mole sauce as was customary in Mexico. Maria Garcia liked to say that her heart was still in Cuernavaca, and she never adapted her cooking. The meal certainly didn't look like the roast-turkey dinner on TV, but when Luis complained, his mother cut him off:

"Next time, you do it," she said.

So Luis started cooking. In eighth grade, he roasted a turkey, and though his mother thought it could use some mole, he was proud of himself. It was admittedly a little dry, but it was a classic American roast turkey.

By high school, Luis was working as a short-order cook at a restaurant next to a bowling alley. The pay was low—five dollars an hour—but for a while, the novelty of making food for people was exciting. Senior year, he found a better job at a place called Doc's Dining & Bar, a place frequented by retirees in Youngtown, a Phoenix suburb. The restaurant was owned by Harold Brunet, who initially hired Luis as a dishwasher. One morning when the kitchen got overwhelmed by retirees looking for French toast and chicken-fried steaks, Luis offered to help out. Brunet was skeptical—Luis rarely spoke and was a bit of a cipher—but when he whipped together a ham-and-cheese omelet, Brunet was impressed. Over Luis's years of silent observation and TV watching, he had learned a lot.

At the beginning of senior year, Luis enrolled in Fredi's Marine Science Seminar. The class was meant to be an opportunity for seniors to work independently on a yearlong project and really get deep into something. Luis thought it would be an opportunity to do little while still getting credit toward graduation.

Fredi offered the seniors a bunch of possible topics—ocean currents, marine-animal migrations—but he also gave them the choice of working on robotics. Luis was pretty sure he'd fall asleep in class if he had to read anything. He didn't want to get in trouble, so he opted for robotics.

It was also nice that the team seemed to want his help. He didn't know Cristian or Lorenzo, but he knew Oscar—the cadet was hard to miss in his pickle-green uniform—and they had had classes together. Now that Luis and Oscar were both seniors in Fredi's seminar, they saw each other throughout the week, and Oscar was friendly. Many people on campus were intimidated by the combination of Luis's size and silence. But Oscar wasn't scared and treated him like anyone else.

"*Hagámoslo*," he told Luis during class one day. "We can build something great."

Luis nodded and then issued his sole pronouncement on the matter:

"Okay."

IN THE SUMMER of 2003—just before the start of the school year and the trebuchet project—Fredi and Allan traveled to Monterey, California, to learn more about a new robotics competition hosted by the Marine Advanced Technology Education (MATE) Center. The organization was founded in 1997 to encourage students to explore careers in marine technology, from oil-rig construction and military applications to environmental and scientific research. In its first seven years, the center placed 119 students into internships onshore and at sea, but the staff had decided that a competition would be a fun way to entice kids to think about ocean work.

The inaugural event was held in 2002 at the Kennedy Space Center in Florida. Jill Zande, the event organizer, styled it as a reimagining of *The Rime of the Ancient Mariner*, Samuel Coleridge's poem. In the original poem, a crew member shoots an albatross that simply wants food and a safe place to land. The killing brings doom upon his ship, conveying the message that those looking for refuge shouldn't be persecuted, as they may often bring good fortune. Zande constructed a parallel narrative, in which a sailor who brings doom upon his ship challenges students with remotely operated vehicles (ROVs) to retrieve his sunken treasure.

"But this I tell / To you, your ROV, and 12-volt battery," the sailor intoned in the competition mission statement. "Those who pursue marine technology careers / Will find wealth beneath the sea."

Zande brought on big-league sponsors, including NASA, the

National Science Foundation, and the Office of Naval Research. The hope was to inspire a new generation of astronauts, scientists, and explorers, and Zande was an enthusiastic evangelist. Part of the challenge was to recruit new students, so Zande created a summer program for teachers. She sent e-mails to Dean Kamen's FIRST teams around the country, and her note caught Allan's attention. It was a great chance to combine marine science with robotics. It was also a free trip somewhere, and teachers rarely get free trips.

The weeklong event in Monterey, California, felt like a vacation. Fredi and Allan were traveling on their own and had no obligation to look like responsible, serious adults. For Allan, it was an opportunity to be a boy again. At home, he was a father to three teenage girls. His wife and a couple of female cats rounded out the family: he was a guy in a house filled with women. For Fredi, it was a break from the unpredictable joys and daily strain of raising one boy with autism and another with Asperger's. There wasn't a lot of time for friendship in his life. Spending time palling around with another teacher was nice.

After the summer, Fredi called Allan so often, his wife, Debbie, would hold her hand over the phone and shout, "It's your other wife." The guys talked about the trebuchet, and the upcoming FIRST competition, and increasingly about ROVs. Part of the purpose of the summer workshop had been to prepare teachers to start their own underwater-robotics team.

"It's kind of ridiculous to think that we'd start an underwater-robotics team in the middle of the desert," Fredi said, laughing on the phone one night. "All the other teams who've competed are from the coasts."

Allan agreed: they had no business doing it. Their kids were poor and had little chance of raising significant money. Plus, they really had no idea what they were doing.

"So you want to do it?"

Fredi could almost hear Allan smiling. "Yeah, let's do it."

TWO

Korvetten-kapitan Wolf Henne stood on the bridge of his sur-
faced U-boat anxiously scanning the sky for American air
patrols.

THE MISSION STATEMENT for the 2004 MATE Robotics Competition was a significant upgrade from the inaugural event's brief riff on *The Rime of the Ancient
Mariner*. For this third iteration, Jill Zande had gotten more ambitious and worked with the authors Vickie Jensen and Harry
Bohm to create a twenty-two-page short story that fictionalized
the demise of *U-157*, a U-boat that had been torpedoed in the
Caribbean in 1942. During the contest, students would explore a
mock-up of the submarine in a swimming pool. The story was
meant to fire their imagination, and Fredi had asked the teens to
read it at home.

Lorenzo read the story in his bedroom. There were funny-
sounding German words and something about a secret agent.
Eventually, the German submarine is engulfed by a mysterious
explosion off the coast of Florida. The captain is then miracu-
lously rescued by a Spanish-speaking fisherman named Pedro
Sanchez.

"Whoa, whoa, whoa," Lorenzo said to himself. Submarines,
explosions—all that was fine. But the mention of Pedro Sanchez
caught his attention.

The next day in class, Lorenzo had a question for Fredi: "So a Mexican saved this guy's life?"

"I don't know if he's Mexican," Fredi said. "He's probably Cuban, since it's Florida."

"They'll probably say the Mexican sank the sub and put him in jail," Lorenzo joked.

Fredi wanted to focus on the robot building and tried to steer the group back to the mission. He ticked off the required tasks. The contest would feature a mock-up of the submarine in a pool on the University of California, Santa Barbara, campus. There were seven tasks. Contestants had to build an ROV that could measure the sub's length, calculate its depth, and navigate inside the structure to recover the captain's bell. The ROV also had to recover two "lost" pieces of research equipment, sample liquid out of the secret-cargo barrels, and determine the temperature of water seeping from a cold-water spring.

Lorenzo just chuckled. There was no way they could do any of that. Even Cristian seemed daunted. Luis just looked blankly at the others without saying anything.

Only Oscar was enthusiastic: "We can do this. We just have to start working on it."

"We live in the desert," Lorenzo said. "We don't even have a pool to practice in."

"We can talk to Scuba Sciences," Fredi said. As a marine science magnet program, Carl Hayden offered scuba certification through Scuba Sciences, a local dive shop with an indoor pool. "I bet they'd let us come in."

Lorenzo didn't seem convinced. Fredi and Allan glanced at each other. They appreciated Oscar's enthusiasm, but this would be a difficult undertaking. They were excited to go to Santa Barbara and check out the event. They'd get to see how other, more sophisticated teams operated. They'd learn a lot and be able to apply the lessons to future years. But they feared that the kids might not be able to handle the challenge. They didn't want to admit it, but both teachers thought their kids might well build a robot that would simply sink to the bottom of the pool and short out.

It was a problem. The last thing either teacher wanted was to make their kids feel bad about themselves. The whole point was to give the guys a chance to accomplish something beyond what they thought possible. But if they showed up at the event and failed utterly, it would only reinforce the impression that they didn't belong in the contest in the first place. That could leave a kid such as Lorenzo with a permanent sense of inferiority.

"We sure about this?" Allan asked when he and Fredi had a moment after school.

Fredi was troubled too. The event overview noted that the third-annual ROV competition "promises to be one of the most technically challenging to date." The competition would be split into two classes: Ranger and Explorer. The Ranger class was geared toward high school teams; the Explorer class was aimed at colleges. "The Explorer class is suitable for those who are willing to design and construct an advanced, multifunctional ROV with a sophisticated control and payload system," read the competition overview. "Explorer class vehicles have a higher power limit, and are usually more costly to build."

But even the Ranger division sounded intimidating. "This class is by far the most popular with high school students," the event materials said. "But don't be fooled. The Ranger class mission tasks are equally as challenging." In 2003, the high school division featured schools such as Milton Academy, the New England private school for high achievers, and Cambridge Rindge & Latin, another Boston-area school, with a 350-year history of excellence. There was even a college that competed at the high school level: the College of the Mainland in Texas City, Texas, was next to Galveston Bay and the Gulf of Mexico, an area with a long history of ocean exploration. It didn't seem fair.

"Wait a second," Fredi said, an idea forming. "If colleges can enter the high school division, why can't high schools enter the college division?"

"MIT is in that division," Allan pointed out.

"But we're not going to win either way," Fredi said. "So why don't we get beat by colleges instead of high schools? That way the kids can say they lost to MIT. There's no dishonor in that."

Allan nodded. He had to admit it had a certain logic.

THE TEACHERS LAID out their plan at the next team meeting. This would be everyone's first year competing in an underwater-robotics event. They were at a real disadvantage, but they had a choice of whom they could lose to.

"Would you rather get beat by a bunch of high schoolers or by MIT?" Fredi asked.

"Who's MIT?" Oscar said. None of the students had heard of the university.

"It's the best engineering school in the country," Allan said. "Maybe even the world."

"It's basically a school filled with Cristians," Fredi said.

"So it's like a school for dorks?" Lorenzo quipped.

"Shut up," Cristian snapped.

Luis watched in bemused silence, a slight grin on his face.

"You want us to go up against the best school in the country?" Oscar asked, still trying to get his mind around the idea.

"We want you to have a good time and learn a lot," Fredi said. "And if you're in the mix with MIT, you'll probably learn more than you would from lesser teams."

"I'm not going to enter something to lose," Oscar said. After his years as a standout ROTC cadet had failed to lead to a career in the military, he didn't want to waste his time again.

"Then let's work hard and build a great robot," Allan said.

"What are our chances of doing well?" Oscar asked.

"We can aim to not finish last," Fredi said, trying to be realistic. "That'll be a good goal."

Lorenzo giggled. "That can be like our motto: 'Don't finish last.'"

THE IDEA OF finishing last didn't sit well with Oscar. At the team's first design meeting in November 2003, he took charge: "We're gonna kick butt, okay?"

Lorenzo laughed until Oscar's stare shut him up. Oscar started going over the description of the contest. MATE's official introduction to the Explorer class mission began with a quotation from Gen. George S. Patton: "Accept the challenges so that you may feel the exhilaration of victory."

Oscar liked that. He was ready, even if the others weren't, and he was determined to drag them along with him.

The third paragraph of the mission statement also made an impact: "This is an exploration mission. Exploration means discovery of the new—and the unexpected. This competition will push your imagination and technical skills. Enter the event with the spirit of the men and women explorers who have set out into the unknown." The event organizers may not have been thinking about four boys from a ghetto high school, but the words resonated.

One of the first tasks was figuring out how they were going to pay for it all. MATE would cover meals and housing in Santa Barabara and provided one hundred dollars for building supplies. That was about enough to cover the cost of driving to California. They were going to need a lot more than that, so Fredi printed up brochures that explained that anybody who donated to the club would get a dollar-for-dollar Arizona state tax deduction. Lorenzo didn't really understand what he was talking about. All he heard was that Fredi wanted him to ask people for money.

"I don't know anybody with money," Lorenzo said.

"Ask your family," Fredi said.

Lorenzo laughed. "They don't got nothing."

Still, Lorenzo took some brochures and asked an older cousin to donate. She had a job cleaning motel rooms and might have some spare cash. "I'm going to be competing in an underwater-robotics competition," he told her.

Lorenzo was known as a jokester in his family, and this was probably one of the weirdest requests the family had ever heard. The cousin refused to donate.

Cristian didn't have any better luck. His parents couldn't spare any money, so he phoned uncles and aunts in California and southern Arizona. They said they'd think about it and never sent anything in.

Surprisingly, Luis made some early progress. One day, after work at Doc's, he approached his boss, Harold, and handed him a robotics brochure. Harold was astonished to learn that his giant, taciturn short-order cook was involved in a NASA-sponsored underwater-robotics contest. "I didn't see that coming," he said and wrote out a check for a hundred dollars.

Oscar tried a similar approach: he stopped by Quality Bedding, the mattress factory that his father worked at. Oscar had spent his summers assembling box frames alongside his dad, so he knew the owner, Iris Oroz, and many of the employees. He handed a brochure to Oroz and explained that West Phoenix was going up against the best of the best. They needed local support if they were going to have a shot. His pitch resonated: Oroz wrote a check for four hundred dollars, and an employee chipped in another four hundred.

That gave them a budget of about nine hundred dollars. It wasn't much, but to four teens from West Phoenix it seemed like an extravagant amount of money to spend on a robot. Now that they had some funding, they began talking about building the robot. The team started by breaking apart a small trebuchet they'd made during the pumpkin-hurling contest. They wanted to figure out how big their ROV needed to be to accommodate propellers, sensors, and controls. They used the two-by-one lumber to make a simple box structure. Once it was done, they stood around the awkward wooden model in the robotics closet and talked through the tasks they were going to have to complete. The first: measure the depth and length of the mocked-up submarine.

Lorenzo pictured the submarine underwater and thought of the simplest possible approach: a length of string. If their ROV could stretch the string from one end to the other, they could measure it. Similarly, they could lower the string from the surface until it touched the bottom of the pool and get a depth reading that way. He proposed the idea to the group.

"And what if it doesn't reach the bottom?" Cristian pointed out. It seemed like a stupid idea.

Lorenzo thought about it for a second. "Yeah, that's a flaw."

The group continued brainstorming, but Lorenzo kept thinking about string. After a minute, he came up with a new approach: "Hey, what if we hung a string down from a floating thing. We could draw markings on it every foot and use a camera to see how far down it went."

This time, it took Cristian a minute to shoot the idea down: "The string could get caught in the propellers. And we're penalized if we leave anything behind in the pool, so we'd waste time trying to retrieve it."

Lorenzo looked disappointed. He thought he was on to something.

"But it wasn't a terrible idea," Cristian allowed.

Lorenzo brightened. "What about just using a tape measure? We can tie a loop onto the end, hook it on to the submarine, and drive the robot backward. The tape will just roll out."

"How do we read it?" Oscar asked.

"Aim a camera at it," Lorenzo said. "We can read it off the video monitor."

"That could work," Oscar said.

Lorenzo flushed with pride. He rarely got compliments for his ideas. He was used to standing behind his godfather and brother, watching them come up with all the cool ideas while they worked on cars. He was expected to silently observe. Now he had a chance to contribute and it felt good.

"It won't work for depth though," Cristian pointed out. "There's nothing at the bottom of the pool to hook on to."

They decided that they'd need two solutions. Lorenzo's tape measure would work for the sub's length, but they'd need something else to gauge depth. They talked about using a scuba-diving computer—they might be able to borrow one from the dive shop—but its margin of error was too big for the precision measurements they were required to make.

"What about a laser tape measure?" Oscar asked. He had worked with his brother on a construction site and seen people using devices that could pinpoint a distance just by aiming a laser beam at an object.

"Will it work underwater?" Cristian asked.

Oscar didn't know. He'd never used one himself.

"You guys should call somebody," Fredi advised. "The best way to figure something out is to call an expert."

Lorenzo was pretty sure nobody would help them, and Luis was obviously not going to make any calls. He barely talked to his teammates. Cristian felt he could figure it out on his own given time. It wasn't a great attitude to have when asking for help, so Oscar decided to make the calls.

He started by googling laser tape measures and quickly came across a company called Distagage in Marathon, Florida. The company specialized in lasers that could read distance as far as 330 feet with an accuracy of an eighth of an inch. Some units could even measure the slope and length of a roof from the ground. The site noted that their top-of-the-line device was "used by more construction professionals around the world than any other brand."

"Sounds expensive," Lorenzo said.

He was right. Models sold for $375 to $725 each. It seemed pointless to even consider them, but Fredi encouraged Oscar to call anyway. "Just ask for advice," Fredi said.

Greg De Tray answered Oscar's call in a mold-infested condo in Miami, Florida. He had only recently formed Distagage and still worked as an insurance adjuster. He had been sent to New York after 9/11, set up shop in Texas after hailstorms pelted the state, and was now in Florida helping Allstate deal with a massive outbreak of residential mold claims. He specialized in catastrophes.

"Distagage," he said, pulling his mask down. "How can I help you?"

De Tray had never intended to get into the laser range finder business. Initially, he had just bought one for himself because the mold-filled rooms he inspected were often nauseating and gave him headaches. The last thing he wanted to do was clamber over damp furniture with a tape measure. A laser range finder was an ideal solution: he didn't have to move around much, and it allowed him to take fast measurements.

His wife and mother-in-law were also in the catastrophe adjustment business, so he decided to buy them range finders as well. But, when he called Leica, the device's Swiss manufacturer, the representative told him that they no longer sold to individuals, only large distributors.

"I'm six feet tall and one hundred and eighty pounds," De Tray said. "How big do I need to be?"

The sales rep laughed and told De Tray that he'd need to buy at least fifty. It was far beyond what most individuals wanted. But the salesman underestimated De Tray, who bristled at rules and noncreative thinking. De Tray spontaneously wrote a check for about ten thousand dollars and bought himself fifty devices. Now, when he rolled from disaster to disaster, he pulled a six-foot-by-twelve-foot cargo trailer loaded with laser range finders and sold them to whoever wanted an extremely precise Swiss-made measuring device.

But he'd never gotten a call from a high schooler. Oscar explained that he was part of the Carl Hayden robotics team in Phoenix, Arizona. They were building an ROV to compete at a competition sponsored by NASA and needed to measure depth underwater. "We were thinking about buying a laser tape measure from Home Depot," Oscar said.

"Those are pieces of crap," De Tray said. He didn't feel that they were really laser range finders. They had a laser, but it was only to show where the thing was pointed. The actual range finding was done acoustically and often provided faulty readings. Those so-called laser range finders gave the whole industry a bad name. "So definitely don't get one of those."

"Do your range finders work underwater?" Oscar asked.

"That's a good question." De Tray was intrigued by this mature-sounding kid from the desert. De Tray thought of himself as somebody willing to take risks (just look at all the range finders he was carting around). Clearly, these kids were also taking chances as well. They seemed similarly ready to try something new, despite what others might think, so he offered to do a test.

That afternoon, he stopped by a Wal-Mart, bought a clear-plastic Tupperware container, and headed for the pool at his Pompano Beach duplex. He put a range finder in the Tupperware, submerged it in the water, and took some readings. It didn't work: the device gave a reading that was clearly wrong. He did it a few times but kept getting the same wrong answer.

At their next team meeting, Oscar called De Tray back and put him on speakerphone. "Sorry to say it, but it doesn't work," De Tray said. "It's giving the wrong answer, but at least it's giving the same wrong answer every time. It's always about 30 percent off."

"The index of refraction!" Cristian blurted.

Everybody turned to look at him.

"What was that?" Lorenzo asked.

"The laser light is traveling through a medium that has a different density than air," Cristian said. He got a blank stare from Lorenzo, who thought Cristian sometimes spoke a different language.

"I get it," Oscar said. "Water is harder to move through than air."

"It moves slower," Cristian said.

"So if we take 30 percent off the readings, it'll give us the right measurement," Oscar said.

"Exactly," Cristian said.

They may have solved the refraction problem, but De Tray's devices still cost hundreds of dollars. But he was impressed. These kids had solved a problem he couldn't solve, and he was supposed to be the expert. He could sense their excitement, and he was excited for them.

He decided to help: "I tell you what. You guys want to use my range finder on your robot, I'll send you one. You can borrow it."

Lorenzo was speechless. Nobody had ever given him anything of significant value before. Nor had he thought that random strangers would be interested in helping him.

Oscar also felt a surge of gratitude. He had a fundamental faith in humanity, though it had been put to the test when the Army turned him down. This was a sign that things were looking up.

"Thank you, sir," Oscar managed to say, trying to keep his emotions in check. "We really appreciate it."

LORENZO RARELY did his homework. He didn't see the point. It seemed like meaningless work to him, so he tended to receive Cs and Ds. He had a GPA of 2.08 at the start of his sophomore year and wasn't too worried. He was having more fun learning about robots than he was in his classes. In fact, all the time he was spending in the robotics closet was distracting him from his regular schoolwork, and his geometry grade dropped to an F.

Fredi could see student grades on the school network and tracked those of the members of the robotics team. The next time he saw Lorenzo, he explained the team's rules: "You know I'm going to have to kick you off the team if you don't get your GPA up?"

"What?" Lorenzo asked, surprised.

"I'll give you till the end of the semester, but if you're not passing all your classes by then, you're off the team."

"For real?"

"For real."

"How do I pass my classes?" Lorenzo asked.

"You do the homework. And sit in the front row. You'll learn more."

Lorenzo decided to start studying. He moved up to the front row in geometry class and began asking the teacher questions. When the homework stumped him, he would bring the workbook to the robotics closet and ask Cristian for the answer.

"No way," Cristian said. "I'll show you the theory, but you have to figure it out for yourself."

Cristian wasn't a great teacher. He didn't have a lot of patience when it came to teaching things he intuitively understood. But Lorenzo turned out to be a perceptive student. To Cristian's surprise, Lorenzo started getting As on geometry tests and his GPA began to climb.

THE COMPETITION'S SECOND task was to measure the temperature of a cold-water spring at the bottom of the pool. To find the thing, contestants were instructed to "look for signs of low-velocity, upward-moving currents," as if that would be easy to do underwater. Once the source was located, the ROV had to extend a temperature sensor into the stream of cold water and report back a reading. They weren't going to be able to hover in place for long, so they needed a thermometer that could take precise and rapid measurements.

Oscar tracked down a supplier in Stamford, Connecticut, that specialized in temperature measuring. When it was founded in 1962, Omega Engineering only offered a single product line of thermocouples. Now it carried more than a hundred thousand products, including baffling-sounding instruments such as the "general-purpose air velocity transducer" ($882) and an "electromagnetic flowmeter" ($2,500). It was hard to make sense of it all, so Oscar dialed the company's 800 number and asked to speak to someone about thermometers.

The operator put him through to Frank Swankoski, a temperature engineer at the company. Swankoski knew as much about thermometer applications as anyone. All day long, he talked to military contractors, industrial engineers, and environmental consultants, so he was momentarily confused when he heard Oscar's high-pitched Mexican accent on the other end of the line. The seventeen-year-old wanted advice on how to build a complex underwater robot.

This was the second call Swankoski had received from amateur roboticists in less than a month. A few weeks earlier, some college oceanic-engineering students had called and said they were entering the national underwater-ROV championships. Oscar explained that his team, too, was competing. They were going up against colleges such as MIT, so they needed to learn as much as they could from the experts. Swankoski liked Oscar's attitude. The college students had simply ordered what they wanted and hung up. Oscar told him they didn't know exactly how best to measure temperature underwater and needed his advice. Oscar activated the speakerphone, so the others could hear anything he might say.

For Swankoski, it was a fun break from the day-to-day grind of the office. Plus, these kids sounded as if they really wanted to learn, so Swankoski launched into an in-depth explanation of his wares, offering details as if he were letting them in on a little secret. "What you really want," he confided, "is a thermocouple with a cold junction compensator."

Swankoski ran through the science: two different alloys are placed side by side, and their different conductive properties transform temperature into voltage. That's a thermocouple. The amount of voltage generated between the alloys is a sign of how much temperature difference there is. That data can quickly be used to calibrate the outside temperature. It was like a master class in materials science and electrical engineering.

"Whoa," Lorenzo said, feeling suddenly a lot smarter. "That's *badass.*"

Oscar asked him how much the device would cost, and Swankoski offered to donate one. He wanted to see these kids win and, with his help, thought they could do it.

"You know," Swankoski said, "I think you can beat those guys from MIT. Because none of them knows what I know about thermometers."

After they hung up, Oscar looked at each team member pointedly. "You hear that?" he said triumphantly. "We got people believing in us, so now we got to believe in ourselves."

IN NOVEMBER 2003—A FEW WEEKS after the team had begun the ROV project—Fredi loaded up a van with six of his marine science students and headed west. If he was going to teach kids about the ocean, it seemed only right to show them the thing. So Oscar ended up crammed in a middle seat with Luis, who took up most of the bench.

Oscar didn't know Luis that well—no one seemed to. His size and expressionless gaze convinced most people to keep their distance. But Oscar now had a five-hour van ride with Luis's belly crowding the seat. He decided to strike up a conversation. Oscar had used his mattress-factory savings to buy a 1991 Mitsubishi 3000GT, a two-door sports car that he was intensely proud of.

"What do you drive?" he asked Luis.

"An '89 Camaro RS."

It was a serious American muscle car, meant for racing. Oscar was impressed. Luis started talking at length about his car's attributes—it had a red paint job and a 3.05-liter, V-8, TBI engine. He spoke quietly, in a restrained rumble, as if he were accustomed to letting his size do the talking. But once he started talking, he didn't seem shy. It was as if he had never said much simply because no one had ever asked him a question. Oscar liked him even more by the time they got to San Diego.

The ocean was mind-boggling to Oscar and Luis. They had glimpsed it on a previous Marine Science trip to California. Now they dove into the water and were startled to discover that it tasted salty. They were used to freshwater lakes and rivers.

Fredi had arranged for the students to tour SeaBotix, a San

Diego–based ROV manufacturer. Company president Donald Rodocker had helped establish the Navy's saturation diving program, which allowed divers to descend beyond one thousand feet using equipment similar to that of scuba divers. After Rodocker left the Navy, he pioneered the commercialization of small ROVs in the eighties with the HyBall ROV, a bright yellow sphere with a clear-plastic midsection that allowed a camera to rotate 360 degrees. To the ROV community, Rodocker was a legend.

Rodocker took the students into the company's laboratory and showed them his latest vehicle, an amazingly compact orange robot called the LBV, which stood for "little benthic vehicle." The machine could dive five hundred feet and cruise at 2.3 miles per hour underwater. The base model retailed for more than ten thousand dollars and rose from there with add-ons.

Despite its diminutive size, the bot still had to contend with a problem endemic to ROVs: its tether. All ROVs are connected to the surface via a bundle of cables that allows its operator to control propellers, sensors, and manipulators. The cables also carry video and infrared signals so that the operator can see where the ROV is going. Normally, the tether also supplies power to the robot. It's a major engineering challenge to minimize the size of those cables, as the combined diameter creates drag, slowing the ROVs movements. It also poses a significant snagging hazard.

Rodocker was a precise man. He wore a neatly trimmed, gray goatee, round spectacles, and a green plaid shirt. Oscar stood just to his left and marveled at the facility. The place was a dream. Racks held specially designed mechanical grippers, endless spools of wire and cable, and beautifully molded plastic casings for the LBV.

While Rodocker talked about building advanced ROVs, Oscar leaned in close to the LBV. An arm sticking out the front had a pincer capable of grabbing a variety of objects. It would be the perfect tool to complete two of their mission tasks: they had to recover the U-boat captain's bell and retrieve a "towfish," a mock-up of a sonar device that would be lying on the pool bottom. Rodocker talked about the prototypes they'd built of the pincer in order to arrive at the final production model. It took a lot of work to make something that was small and highly functional.

Emboldened by his experiences talking to De Tray and Swankoski, Oscar blurted out a question that would have been unthinkable weeks earlier: "Sir, would you consider lending us one of your prototypes if you aren't using it anymore?"

"I'd be happy to," Rodocker responded easily.

On the drive back to Phoenix, the kids marveled at their good fortune. They had a state-of-the-art pincer on loan from a real ROV company. They'd learned how salty the ocean is. Oscar and Luis had become fast friends. The trip had been a great success.

But then a problem appeared in the heat waves coming off the I-10. Near Yuma, Arizona, just after they'd left California, they spotted brake lights. Cars were coming to a stop. A phalanx of official vehicles bore the logo of Immigration and Customs Enforcement. They were headed into an immigration checkpoint.

Everybody's heart rate kicked up. Luis had a green card thanks to his father, but Oscar was in the country illegally. He knew what had happened to the Wilson High kids in Niagara Falls the previous summer. He could be arrested and deported.

"Give me your school IDs," Fredi commanded. "And nobody talk besides me. Understood?"

The kids nodded and nervously handed their IDs forward. Fredi eased up to the checkpoint and rolled down his window. An officer asked for identification. Fredi handed over the school IDs. "We're on a school trip," Fredi offered.

The agent glanced at the van—it bore the school's name. He could see the Latino kids sitting inside. Oscar prepared for the worst. He imagined being torn from his family and dropped across the border. He wouldn't know what to do or where to go.

The agent scrutinized the IDs and looked back at the kids. After a moment, he handed the IDs back.

"Okay, have a good trip," he said and waved them on.

Fredi accelerated before the guy could change his mind. Nobody talked for a while. Suddenly, their desire to see the ocean and learn about robots seemed foolish and maybe even reckless.

OSCAR RETURNED to the robotics closet with a mix of excitement and fear. The anxiety he felt at the immigration checkpoint had dissipated, but the threat was still there. He had to decide. The ROV contest was back in California. If he wanted to compete, he'd have to risk another checkpoint.

Oscar made a quick decision. In ROTC, he had done multiple rope courses, rappelling down sheer cliffs. He'd learned to not let his fear control him. This was no different. If he wanted to do something great, he'd have to put his worries aside. They now had a thermocouple, a range finder, and a frightening black claw that only an engineer could love. Oscar picked the pieces up and positioned them in the wooden model.

"I think we can fit everything," he said.

With that, he put the checkpoint behind him.

Soon, Cristian and Lorenzo showed up, and the kids started to talk about how to build the real ROV. Fredi and Allan knew that other teams had used machined metal in previous years. Some colleges had machine shops and could custom-fabricate parts. Machined-metal ROVs tended to be smaller and more compact, which came in handy when exploring cramped underwater spaces. But Carl Hayden couldn't afford the necessary metal, nor did the students have access to a machine shop. Even if they did, nobody knew how to operate the machines.

"We should use glass syntactic flotation foam," Cristian said excitedly. "It's got a really high compressive strength. They use it on submersibles."

Lorenzo didn't really know what *submersibles* meant. Cristian, however, had done his research. He had watched James Cameron's *Ghosts of the Abyss*, a documentary about the director's journey twelve thousand feet down to visit the wreck of the *Titanic*. The film crew used two ROVs outfitted with glass syntactic foam to enter the wreck. Cristian had taken this hint and done further research online.

"It's got glass microspheres embedded in an epoxy resin so it keeps it shape under pressure while still providing buoyancy," Cristian said.

"Damn, dude, how do you come up with all that?" Lorenzo said.

"How much is it?" Oscar asked.

"Two, maybe three thousand for what we need," Cristian responded.

"*¿Cuánto?*" Lorenzo blurted. It was a lot of money.

Cristian tended to think in abstract, idealized solutions. They didn't have that kind of money and everyone knew it. They had a total budget of less than a thousand dollars. Glass syntactic foam was not an option.

One alternative was polyvinyl chloride, or PVC. It was a material they were all familiar with. For decades, migrant laborers had installed PVC pipes throughout American farmlands. Workers from Mexico and Central America laid miles of the white plastic tube to irrigate fields of strawberries and corn. The piping didn't have the strength of metal, but, like the laborers, it was low cost, easy to work with, and rugged. The combination had helped turn America into an agricultural juggernaut, so it seemed only natural to use it now. It was also all they could afford.

"We can run wires through the pipe to keep them dry," Lorenzo said. "And the air inside will make it float."

It seemed like an idea worth testing, so Luis drove to Home Depot and bought twenty dollars worth of three-centimeter-diameter Schedule 40 PVC piping. Schedule 40 pipe was an unassuming subset of PVC, but it had impressive attributes. It was strong enough to work in temperatures as high as 140 degrees and able to withstand pressure 250 feet below the surface. They'd only be going down fifteen feet, so it was more than robust enough for the job.

When they gathered around the ten-foot-long pipes in the robotics closet, it seemed like a lot of material. "There'll be a lot of air in there," Oscar pointed out.

Cristian started scribbling on a piece of paper and made a crude sketch of an ROV. While the others watched, he calculated the volume of air inside the pipes and concluded that they would need some ballast.

"You mean like something heavy?" Lorenzo asked.

"Yeah," Cristian said, his tone suggesting it was obvious what ballast was.

The simplest solution was to affix weights to the frame to counterbalance the buoyancy. But weights would take up precious space in a machine already cluttered with sensors, propellers, and a pincer. The machine would turn into an unwieldy behemoth. To further complicate matters, they would have to contend with the thick tether cable sprouting out the top.

"Wait," Cristian said, an idea forming. "What if we put the battery on board?"

It was a bold idea. Most teams wouldn't consider putting their power supply in the water. A small leak could take the whole system down. But the competition required agile movements through narrow passages; a thinner tether would be a key advantage. Cristian proposed housing the battery in a heavy, waterproof case at the bottom of the ROV, where it would stabilize the machine's movements. An onboard battery would also limit transmission loss. Voltage dropped if it had to travel down a long cable. If the battery was right next to the propellers, that wasn't a problem, and they wouldn't have to run a thick electrical cable to the bot.

"What do you think?" Cristian asked the group.

"That's a badass idea," Lorenzo said, his highest compliment.

Oscar was worried though: "There's a reason other people don't do it."

"If we do the same as everyone else, we'll finish last because they've done it before," Cristian fired back.

"If our ROV short-circuits, we'll definitely finish last," Oscar said.

"Sure, but if we can't figure out how to waterproof a case, then we shouldn't be in an underwater contest," Cristian said.

"He's got a point," Luis said abruptly.

Everybody looked at Luis. He looked calmly back at everyone else. It was as if the oracle had spoken.

"Okay, then," Oscar said. "Let's put the battery on board."

FOR LORENZO, the robotics team was like a new family. In some respects, Fredi and Allan were surrogate parents, constantly advising him and pushing him to do better. It was the same for the others. A team spirit had developed. Lorenzo wasn't the only one sitting in the front row of his classes. The rest of the team had adopted the approach as well. "What's the point of doing something half-assed," Fredi told them repeatedly. The boys took that to heart.

It wasn't a perfect family. Cristian tended to look down on ideas that weren't his own; Oscar wasn't convinced that Lorenzo was reliable; and Luis showed little emotion of any kind. But the guys at least listened to Lorenzo, let him brainstorm crazy ideas, and didn't tell him to go away because he looked funny. The robotics closet felt more like home than his actual house. Fredi and Allan joked that, if they let him, Lorenzo would be happy living in the cramped room.

But that wasn't possible. Lorenzo stayed as late as he could after school, but both Fredi and Allan had a forty-five-minute drive back to their families in East Phoenix. Fredi was already asking a lot of Pam; she was supportive of his work, but she also needed all the help she could get at the end of a long day at home with the boys. Lorenzo usually lingered until Fredi shut off the lights and started locking the doors.

Fridays were the hardest. Lorenzo's dad was likely to start drinking Milwaukee's Best, and Fredi and Allan weren't always able to come back to school over the weekend. That meant two days of hell.

The school week was only a partial respite. Lorenzo was making headway with Cristian, Oscar, and Luis, but the rest of the school still seemed to view him as a misshapen freak. He wanted to look cool and started wearing jewelry: two gold earrings in his left ear, a gold chain with a medallion, and a flashy metal watch. But as he passed people in the hall, they still laughed. Somehow he continued to strike his classmates as a walking joke.

The taunting increased as his sophomore year got under way. One day, in health class, a kid behind him started teasing him about his hair. *It's girly; he looks like a woman.* Lorenzo ignored the guy. Then Lorenzo felt something hit the back of his head. The student had flicked a wad of gum into his long hair. Lorenzo tried to pull it out, but it only got more entwined. The class snickered. He was mortified; he had gum stuck on his fingers and in his hair, and he could hear his classmates trying to suppress their laughter.

When he got home that night, he burst into tears. His mother offered to cut the gum out; that would be the fastest solution. But Lorenzo refused; he didn't want somebody to be able to force him to cut his hair. His mother quietly got some vegetable oil and started trying to loosen the gum. It took three days for her to get it all out.

Soon after the gum incident, Lorenzo was trailed home by another student. As he crossed over the Thirty-Fifth Avenue overpass, the student started asking Lorenzo why he was wearing earrings and a flashy watch. Lorenzo ignored him for a while, but the kid kept pestering him. Lorenzo finally stopped and turned.

"This is how I am," he said.

"But you look stupid," the kid said.

Lorenzo tried using his anger-management techniques. "*Diez, nueve, ocho, siete . . . ,*" he counted backward. He knew that if he got in another fight, he could be expelled. Before, he might not have cared. Now he wanted to build this robot.

Luis Aranda, Oscar Vazquez, Lorenzo Santillan, and Cristian Arcega (*bottom*, from left) in June 2004 at the Marine Advanced Technology Education Robotics Competition in Santa Barbara, California (Courtesy of Faridodin Lajvardi)

Fredi Lajvardi mentored the robotics team at Carl Hayden Community High School in Phoenix. (Courtesy of Faridodin Lajvardi)

Allan Cameron in the 1980s, when he first became a teacher
(Courtesy of Allan Cameron)

Luis (*left*) was a quiet giant in high school, while Oscar (*right*) was a standout cadet in the Junior Reserve Officer Training Corps. (LEFT: courtesy of Luis Arranda; RIGHT: courtesy of Oscar Vazquez)

Lorenzo in the lab (Courtesy of Faridodin Lajvardi)

Cristian shows his mother the robot he helped build for the Arizona FIRST (For Inspiration and Recognition of Science and Technology) regionals.
(Courtesy of Faridodin Lajvardi)

Cristian and Lorenzo working on Stinky, their underwater ROV, at Carl Hayden
(Courtesy of the author)

From left: Oscar, Luis, Lorenzo, Allan,
Cristian, and Fredi with Stinky in 2004
(Courtesy of Faridodin Lajvardi)

From left: Lorenzo, Luis, Oscar, and Cristian in Philadelphia in 2005, in
front of the Liberty Bell (Courtesy of Faridodin Lajvardi)

From left: Allan, Luis, Lorenzo, Oscar, Cristian, and Fredi in 2010, when Oscar returned to the United States after having deported himself (Courtesy of the author)

Stinky
(Courtesy of Faridodin Lajvardi)

The kid behind him didn't let up. He started saying things about Lorenzo's mom and Lorenzo tensed. He couldn't allow anybody to insult his mother.

"*Hijo de puta*," the boy said. Your mother's a whore.

Lorenzo snapped. He hurled himself at the boy. He managed to land a few punches, but the kid walloped him in the face, bruising Lorenzo's eye socket. Traffic on the bridge came to a stop. Someone separated the boys.

When he got home, his dad noticed his swollen eye and demanded to know who hit him. Lorenzo didn't want to say.

"Tell me and I'll kick his ass," his father said.

It was the most his father had offered to do for him in a long time. Lorenzo felt a swirl of emotion. He didn't want to get into fights, but at least his dad expressed concern when he did. It seemed possible that if he fought more, his dad would pay more attention to him. His dad didn't seem to care about Lorenzo's interest in robotics. Lorenzo wondered if he was trying to be something other than what he was. Maybe he was never meant to be anything more than an impoverished immigrant who brawled his way through life.

News of the fight spread around school the next day, and Lorenzo was called into Principal Steve Ybarra's office. Lorenzo had been warned not to fight again, so Ybarra had the option of expelling him.

Lorenzo didn't know what to say or how to act. He just felt lost. "I'm sorry" was all he could say.

Ybarra knew that if he kicked Lorenzo out of school, he'd probably gravitate toward the gangs. If Ybarra let him stay, Lorenzo would be able to continue working on the robotics team. The support of teachers—notably Fredi—might turn the kid around. Ybarra decided to take a chance and assigned Lorenzo to a second round of anger-management courses.

Fredi tracked Lorenzo down between classes later that day. "Come with me," Fredi said angrily. Lorenzo dutifully followed him back to the robotics closet.

"You've got to stop this," Fredi told him when they got there.

"What was I supposed to do? He was insulting my mother."

"You know, I got beat up in high school too," Fredi said, remembering the early eighties, when he was targeted for being Iranian. It wasn't a pleasant memory.

"For real?" Lorenzo couldn't imagine an authority figure like Fredi being attacked.

"They want you to get angry. So if you give that to them, they win."

To Fredi, this was a battle for the future of an unusual but talented kid. He appreciated Lorenzo's offbeat ideas and felt that the long-haired goofball had genuine talent. But Lorenzo was caught in the tractor-beam pull of poverty and low expectations. They were powerful forces to contend with. It wasn't hard to imagine Lorenzo's dropping out. He wouldn't have many opportunities after that. Getting involved with WBP, his cousins' gang, was one obvious option.

Fredi had once been an oddball kid too. He'd wanted to build hovercrafts and didn't get along with his parents. When Fredi was in college, he took a physics class over the summer at a local community college. At the time, his younger brother, Ali, was a straight-A student at the University of California, San Diego, and Ali taunted Fredi for attending what he viewed as a lesser school. Fredi warned him repeatedly to stop. When the mockery continued, Fredi punched his brother in the face, giving him a bloody nose.

So Fredi could understand how Lorenzo was feeling. He also knew that anger rarely led to positive outcomes. The brothers hadn't talked for a year after the altercation. That wasn't what Fredi wanted, nor did he want Lorenzo to make the same mistakes.

He decided to offer Lorenzo a novel solution: "Next time somebody wants to fight you, pretend you're having a seizure." Fredi simulated having a seizure, contorting himself and shaking violently. "Like that."

Lorenzo broke into a sly smile. The image of his teacher writhing on the floor to get out of a beating made Lorenzo giggle. He usually felt like the weirdest person in the room, but now Fredi was challenging him for the title.

"You gotta do something, right?" Fredi asked.

The humor helped take a weight off Lorenzo. He realized he was never going to be the ass-kicking brawler his father might want him to be. He couldn't be anything other than what he was: a sweet kid with an unorthodox perspective. It was a perspective that lined up surprisingly well with Fredi's.

"I'm serious," Fredi said. "Just flop around on the ground. They'll leave you alone."

"Okay. I'll do that," Lorenzo said.

Then he erupted into real laughter. It felt good.

THE ROV'S THIRD task was going to be the hardest. According to the backstory, the U-boat sank while it was carrying thirteen mysterious barrels. Now, competition organizers explained, those barrels were leaking. It posed an "environmental danger" that needed to be quickly assessed. The robots would have to locate the barrel, insert a probe into a half-inch pipe, and extract a five-hundred-milliliter sample, all while hovering underwater. Oscar and Cristian were pretty sure the task would be impossible to complete, so they assigned it to Lorenzo. If he failed, they figured it wouldn't set them back much, since it probably wasn't doable in the first place. It would allow the rest of the team to focus on the more easily accomplished goals.

The other teams in the Explorer class brought a wealth of engineering prowess to the sampling problem. MIT considered using vacuum containers and a screw-activated syringe before settling on a series of submersible bladders joined by a T-valve. Lake Superior State University used an innovative dual-pump system, while Long Beach City College employed a three-way solenoid valve. Lorenzo, left to his own ingenuity, decided to use a balloon.

The humble balloon had a lot to recommend it. Unlike a rigid container, it carried no air when deflated so it wouldn't add buoyancy. Some of the other teams were trying to use rigid containers that had the air vacuumed out. Lorenzo didn't even get to that level of complexity. A balloon was flexible, could expand and contract easily, and cost almost nothing. There was no reason to consider something more complex.

The next problem was how to suction the fluid into the balloon. Fredi suggested using a sump pump. They were often installed in underground basements. If the house flooded, the submerged pump could discharge the water, so he knew they worked well underwater. Fredi was worried that they might cost a lot, but on an exploratory outing to Home Depot with Lorenzo, they found a small twelve-volt pump for thirty-five dollars. Lorenzo also picked up some narrow copper tubing for two dollars.

Back in the robotics closet, Lorenzo started experimenting. He glued PVC fittings to each end of the sump pump. One fitting narrowed the intake section to the size of the copper pipe. He inserted the pipe, glued it in place, and bent it so that it jutted out from the front of the bot like the proboscis of a butterfly.

He pulled a balloon over the other end of the pump. When he plugged it in, the pump sucked up five hundred milliliters of water in twenty seconds. It worked perfectly except that the weight of the water made the balloon fall over. It wouldn't be a problem underwater—the balloon wouldn't fall over below the surface—but when the ROV was pulled out to retrieve the sample, the balloon would flop to the side, come off the pump, and spill the sample everywhere.

Lorenzo tried affixing the balloon in a variety of ways, but each time the balloon fell over like a drunkard who'd lost his balance. When it did, the balloon popped off and water gushed everywhere. Lorenzo had to keep sopping up the mess. It was getting a little embarrassing, and Lorenzo was already deeply vulnerable to any mockery. Fredi worried that if the team laughed at Lorenzo's mistakes, he might give up.

"You're doing good," Fredi reassured him. "You're getting close."

Lorenzo nodded. He wasn't sure he was getting close to anything but a damp pair of shoes, but Fredi's words made him feel a little better.

"Maybe if I built something to catch it, that could help," Lorenzo said.

"Try it," Fredi said.

Lorenzo fished an empty Coca-Cola liter bottle out of the garbage and hacksawed it in half. He flipped the top half upside down and placed it over the pump so that it served as a sort of catcher's mitt for the balloon. Now the balloon filled inside the container, but the liter bottle was too restricting. As the balloon expanded, it bulged out of the top of the bottle and pulled the balloon off the pump. Water sprayed everywhere.

"Try something bigger than a Coke bottle," Fredi said while Lorenzo glowered. "You're onto something good."

The next day, Lorenzo showed up with an empty gallon-size plastic milk container. Fredi watched Lorenzo hack it in half, affix it to the pump, and turn the system on for twenty seconds. The balloon filled with water and gently leaned over into the molded interior of the milk jug. Lorenzo turned the pump off. The balloon lolled inside the jug, its neck securely fastened around the pump.

Fredi was impressed. It was a practical, cheap, and ingenious solution. At the outset, he hadn't been sure Lorenzo could pull it off. Now that Lorenzo had, Fredi felt a wave of emotion. It seemed possible that the kid might make it through after all.

"You did it," Fredi said, clapping Lorenzo on the shoulder.

Lorenzo responded with a big smile. "I did it."

"¿QUÉ ES ESO?" Lorenzo's mother asked him. She was holding a letter printed in English and wanted to know what it said. Lorenzo scanned it in their living room while his mother waited. It was a foreclosure notice. His mom had recently been laid off from her job cleaning rooms at a Days Inn, and Lorenzo's dad was burning through twelve-packs of Milwaukee's Best on a regular basis.

"*La carta dice que van a perder la casa, tienen que evacuar la casa en treinta días,*" Lorenzo said. The letter says you're going to lose the house, you have to evacuate the house in thirty days.

When Lorenzo was nine years old, the family had scrapped together a meager down payment to buy the house. The mortgage was about six hundred dollars a month. Lorenzo's mother insisted that she'd been paying it, but she didn't have any receipts to prove it. Lorenzo didn't know whom to believe. It felt as if just when things were starting to get better, something always came along to put him back in his place.

Lorenzo shuffled through the other mail and found a letter from a Realtor who advertised his ability to stave off eviction. Lorenzo phoned him and the guy sounded helpful. He said he would talk to the bank and try to negotiate a deal. Lorenzo allowed himself to feel a moment of hope and prayed that the Realtor wasn't a fraud.

OSCAR AND LUIS took on the problem of what propellers to use. Part of the challenge was to figure out how many were needed and how to arrange them. They didn't need to be enormously powerful. In fact, the more power the motors consumed, the quicker it would run down the onboard battery. At first, they reasoned that they would need to be able to go forward, backward, up, and down.

"Three motors should be enough," Oscar said. "Two horizontal to drive and one vertical to go up and down."

"What if we need to tilt to pick something up?" Luis rumbled.

"You're right."

The more they talked, the more complex they realized it was. The robot needed to be able to tip forward if they wanted the mechanical arm to pick up the towfish or the captain's bell. Inside the submarine, the robot would need to move sideways, and that would require another motor. Maneuverability was critical, they concluded, and decided that they'd need five motors total.

Fredi suggested they consider trolling motors, which were used for fishing boats that had to move quietly. He wasn't much of a fisherman—he didn't have time—but he'd seen the motors and knew they were efficient and small enough to fit inside the PVC framework. Typically, they powered aluminum boats and weren't known for their brawn. But when coupled with a relatively lightweight ROV, they would provide a lot of zip.

Oscar googled trolling motors and found a company called

Mercury Marine. Using the phone on Fredi's desk in the marine science classroom, Oscar dialed the 800 number and eventually got through to Kevin Luebke, one of the company's endorsement managers. Normally, Luebke doled out motors to winners of the Bassmaster Classic, guys who liked to talk about shallow-running crankbaits and rocky riprap. Oscar had to explain that they weren't fishermen. They were high school students competing in an underwater-robot contest.

Luebke was charmed and quickly agreed to sell them five discounted motors. Normally, the MotorGuide motors sold for about $100. Luebke marked them down to $75 each. At a total of $375, it was still a big part of the project's budget, but they needed reliable propulsion.

When the motors arrived in the mail, Oscar and Luis gingerly pulled them out of the box. It was like getting a Christmas present and made the project feel even more real. They were shiny and black and had two menacing blades.

The next question was how to arrange them. At Fredi's suggestion, Oscar and Luis filled a marine science sink with water and plopped in a small piece of wood. They took turns moving it around the sink with their fingers and discovered that if they pushed with their fingers at a forty-five-degree angle, they were able to turn the wood much faster than if they simply pushed it directly from behind. Without realizing it, they were discovering the principles of torque. The result of their small-scale sink experiment: a machine that would be able to rotate around a central point with little drift.

Given their limited budget, they decided they wouldn't be able to build a waterproof housing for the robot's control. Instead, they found a discontinued plastic briefcase at a local electronics store. It claimed to be waterproof up to fifty feet. Plus, it was on sale for $120, a bargain. Since the pool in Santa Barbara wouldn't be deeper than fifteen feet, they figured it would be okay. They bought the case, drilled a hole in the side for the wires, plugged it, and submerged the whole thing in one of the marine science room's big sinks. It worked fine, at least in a sink.

Cristian had drawn a detailed plan of the ROV, including the lengths of every segment of PVC pipe that would be needed. Since the pipe came in lengths of ten feet, it would need to be cut into pieces. They had bought a pipe cutter, but Cristian found that he couldn't operate it. The pipe was too thick and Cristian wasn't strong enough.

"*Con ganas,*" Lorenzo teased him. "Squeeze that thing."

"You try it," Cristian shot back, and handed him the cutter.

"*Déjame enseñarte,*" Lorenzo said. "I'll show you how it's done."

Lorenzo clamped down on the thing. He could barely budge it. He tried sitting on it ("That's not gonna count," said Cristian), banging it against a wall ("Don't mess up the wall!" Fredi shouted), and finally succeeded in breaking through the pipe by straining with every ounce of his strength.

"See, I told you it was hard," Cristian said, feeling vindicated.

"Let me try that." Oscar took the cutter from Lorenzo while Luis watched from across the room with a bemused grin. Oscar, squeezing as hard as he could, cut one piece after working on it for five minutes. He could do it—just barely—but his hands ached afterward, and they had to fashion approximately eighty pieces. Everybody looked over at Luis.

"You want to give this a try?" Oscar asked.

Luis lumbered over and took the cutter from Oscar. He fed a piece of pipe into the device and clamped down, cutting the pipe in one smooth movement. Everybody looked at him with awe.

"It's like butter," he said.

It took Luis two days to cut all the pieces. As he sliced through pipe after pipe, Oscar, Lorenzo, and Cristian started joining the sections together without glue to make sure they all fit. Luis did his best to measure the pieces before he cut them, but it was hard to be exact with a hand-powered slicer. Once he was done, they placed the last piece into position and stood back to take a look at their creation. It was a slightly lopsided white plastic frame.

"That looks good," Allan enthused.

"Very cool," Fredi agreed.

In reality, it looked like crap, but there was potential.

A MONTH AFTER the students had begun the ROV project, Dean Kamen released his annual robotics challenge. The small group working on the ROV was just a part of the larger, twenty-odd-member Carl Hayden robotics team. For this broader team, Kamen's event was the main focus. For Oscar, Luis, Lorenzo, and Cristian, it was an opportunity to hone their construction skills on dry land, experience a real competition, and focus on their teamwork. They decided to join the other kids on Kamen's challenge.

It promised to be a lot of fun. Kamen had cooked up something akin to robot basketball. He invited students to build a machine that could range across half a basketball court and collect a variety of balls. For a portion of the game, the machines would run autonomously. The rest of the time, the kids would drive the bots from behind a ten-foot-tall Plexiglas wall. The goal was to place the balls in a tall hamper—a combination of basketball and robot warfare, as machines were pitted against one another in a dash for balls. At the end of the game, teams could earn bonus points if their robot could suspend itself off the ground on a pull-up bar.

Kamen's organization shipped participating teams a box of supplies to jump-start the robot building. The most important part was a robot controller, a compact-but-versatile black square that contained all the processors, connections, and radio controls needed. It packed a programmable processor able to handle ten million instructions per second and could communicate via a tether or radio. It weighed just over half a pound and was about the size of a hand.

One of the first things they had to learn was how to solder. To build a robot, students need to be able to connect wires, so Fredi and Allan showed them all the soldering tricks they'd need to know: how to "tin the tip," how to apply the solder to the wires, and why not to apply solder to the iron itself. After a few practice sessions, the kids were far from being experts, but they were able to forge basic connections.

Still, there was a big difference between soldering a connection and building an entire robot. The idea of assembling a robot that could play basketball was even more forbidding.

"What if we just don't play that game?" Lorenzo suggested.

As usual, Lorenzo's ideas seemed silly at first. The other team members pointed out that the whole point of the competition was to try to play the game, even if it was hard.

"But what if we just do the last thing," he said. "What if we build a robot that does the pull-up and nothing else."

The idea had some merit. While other competitors were racing to grab balls, the Carl Hayden team could have a clear shot at the pull-up bar. A robot that hoisted itself up earned fifty points, the equivalent of gathering ten of the small balls. Plus, they would block other competitors from getting to the bar.

Fredi and Allan thought it was a clever approach. It would be hard to build an offensive robot on the same level as that of the teams who had participated in the FIRST program for years. But they were pretty sure the Carl Hayden kids could build a robot that could do a single pull-up. After all, Oscar did dozens of them every day. He could serve as the model.

They constructed a fiberglass frame and affixed four wheels to it. There was no need for it to be complicated; it had to travel just a little over twenty feet to the pull-up bar. They attached a clip to the top of a broom handle and connected it to a small motor that jerked the handle ten feet into the air. The clip was tied to a rope. When the pole extended up and clipped on to something, they activated a winch that dragged the robot up the rope and into the air.

They arrived at the Arizona regionals in Veterans Memorial Coliseum on March 11, 2004. Many of the thirty-five other teams boasted the kind of technical capabilities that Cristian dreamed of. They could hurl balls through the air and could even operate autonomously. In comparison, the Carl Hayden robot was a broom handle on wheels.

They had problems from the start. In the opening round, the robot's chain slipped off and fell onto the arena floor. While other robots zipped about, their machine sat motionless on the floor. When the round ended, they hustled the bot back to their "pit," an area behind the playing field where they'd set up their tools. The whole team was intensely focused—they only had forty-eight minutes until their next round and didn't have time to take the whole robot apart. They decided to try to repair the chain surgically, with seven team members detaching and lifting various parts. Cristian felt a thrill as everybody got their hands inside the machine. It was like a game of perfectly choreographed Twister.

It worked. They got the chain repositioned and rolled back to the court. When their next round began, their robot rolled straight for the pull-up bar while other robots scampered after the balls. Lorenzo flipped the switch that activated the broom motor. The handle shot up and snapped the clip into place. In a moment, the bot was dangling off the ground. It didn't guarantee them a win— other teams could score more points getting balls—but they ended up winning three out of nine rounds. They also tied two. It was good enough for twenty-first place out of thirty-six teams. Their enthusiasm—if not their technical sophistication—impressed the judges, who awarded them the Engineering Inspiration Award.

It recognized their "success in advancing respect and appreciation for engineering with a team's school and community." Most important, they didn't finish last.

When they got back to their seats in the amphitheater, Fredi and Allan had good news. "Guess what?" Allan said, buzzing with excitement. "That award qualifies you for the national championship. You're going to Atlanta!"

Cristian and Lorenzo were momentarily flummoxed, not because they weren't excited—they were—but because they didn't know where Atlanta was. When Fredi told them they'd have to fly there, they felt a mix of excitement and nervousness. Neither of them had been on a plane before.

When Cristian got home, he told his mother the good news. Leticia was not thrilled. She didn't want her son traveling after what had happened to the Wilson High kids at Niagara Falls. It was an unnecessary risk, and she told him he couldn't go.

Cristian was furious. No way was he going to let a robot he helped build travel to the national championship without him. He asked Fredi to do something, so Fredi called the Arcega home. Fredi explained that he used to coach track and had been traveling with kids for years. He'd never had any problems and intended to keep it that way. He also mentioned that Cristian was becoming an important member of the team. They needed him.

Leticia wasn't swayed, so Fredi tried another tack. He pointed out that if Cristian wanted to find a job in engineering, this was a great way to lay the groundwork. Engineers were in demand and made good money. Competing at a national robotics championship was a valuable experience that would lead to new opportunities. That resonated, and Leticia reluctantly gave her approval.

Five weeks after the regional event, the teens were strapped into an eastbound flight. As the plane taxied onto the runway, it rattled. Annalisa Regaldo, a sophomore sitting next to Lorenzo, told him that the sound was a bad sign: "I think we're gonna crash."

Lorenzo started to panic. "For real?" He looked around for a way out, and Annalisa broke into laughter. She was just kidding.

Lorenzo didn't appreciate the joke. He was pretty sure he didn't understand girls, and this only reinforced that belief. He decided to stick closer to Cristian, Oscar, and Luis.

Oscar, however, was a natural gentleman. On their first night in Atlanta, the teenagers snuck down to the hotel pool, and a game of tag erupted. A girl slipped on the slick surface, conked her head on the edge of the pool, and fell in. While the other kids watched her sink to the bottom, Oscar dove in and pulled her out. He helped her back to her room and sat with her until it was clear she was okay.

When the competition began at the hulkingly large Georgia Dome, the Carl Hayden team's robot seemed as dazed to be there as they were. In an early match, it froze in the middle of the playing field. Visualizing all the potential problems, Cristian calculated that most likely the battery was not sitting right in the robot.

Cristian asked another team for help. "Will you ram us?" he shouted.

"What?" the other robot's driver said.

"Just hit us as hard as you can."

The driver complied, smashing into the Carl Hayden robot. Surprisingly, it worked. The battery slotted into its connectors and the robot started rolling toward the pull-up bar.

Lorenzo hooted and slapped Cristian on the back. "That was *frictastic*."

"What does that even mean?" Cristian said.

Lorenzo smiled. "It means frickin' fantastic."

He was weird, Cristian thought, but sometimes Lorenzo was pretty funny too.

At the end of every day, Fredi and Allan convened a team

meeting in their hotel room. They analyzed everything—from the way Luis unloaded the robot from the crate to the match itself—and asked the kids what had gone well and what needed to be done better. The teachers deliberately stretched the meetings on for hours. They wanted the students to learn as much as possible from the experience, but they also wanted them exhausted. The goal: make the kids so tired, they'd go straight to sleep and not cause problems horsing around all night. The meeting was, in essence, a bedtime story. Fredi would drone on about minutiae until he saw eyes drooping. Then the teachers hustled everybody off to bed.

Though the team ended up placing in the middle of their division—thirty-ninth out of seventy-three teams—the result wasn't bad for a newbie team and far from last place. More important, they had fun. After the closing ceremonies, Fredi and Allan took the kids for a walk around downtown Atlanta. It was hot and muggy, but they felt great. They posed for pictures flexing their muscles, and Oscar organized the group into a three-tier human pyramid in the middle of a public square. Lorenzo clambered onto the second tier, a huge smile on his face. He felt as if he were part of a group of superheroes. Oscar had done this type of group-building exercise in ROTC. Now he was building a new team.

AFTER ATLANTA, the kids had about ten weeks until the ROV championship. Their experience building a ground-based robot proved critical as they set about assembling their underwater vehicle. They were comfortable with the FIRST controller so they decided to use it as the brains of their ROV. Since they now knew how to solder, they could connect the propellers and cameras to the controller. They had also traveled and competed together and employed a shorthand in their conversation. Diagonal cutting pliers were *dykes*, electrical connectors were *Andersons*, and PVC pipe became *elbows* and *T-fittings*.

For Lorenzo, it was like a new kind of gang slang. The group also offered some of the same benefits of being in a gang. Now that he hung out with Luis on campus, Lorenzo found that other students were less likely to make fun of him. Few people wanted to antagonize someone as big as Luis, so the ridicule decreased. It gave Lorenzo some space to figure out whom he wanted to be instead of acting in response to insults.

One of the things he enjoyed most outside of robotics was watching his mother cook. Lorenzo loved the pungent smells of pan-fried ancho and sliced onions and the bubbling steam coming off her boiling beans. She didn't buy chili powder from the store; she ground peppers in a mortar and pestle and used the red flakes to make a spicy salsa. It was somehow reassuring, one of the few things in his life that seemed dependable and comforting, and it made Lorenzo want to learn more about cooking. The robotics team was showing him that there was a lot more to the world than he knew. The same must be true of food.

Unfortunately, Carl Hayden had a single, lackluster cooking class. Among other things, instructors taught students how to use a microwave to make a cake from a box. Lorenzo wasn't impressed. Metro-Tech High, another school in West Phoenix, offered a more robust program. They had a real kitchen and ran a restaurant out of the school. Lorenzo told Fredi that he was thinking about transferring. He loved robotics, but he was also drawn to cooking. It was a hard choice.

"Why does it have to be a choice?" Fredi asked. Lorenzo was just starting to build a new life for himself. Fredi worried that if he left robotics, that foundation would crumble. "Why don't you go to cooking school over the summer?"

"Because that costs money."

"How much?"

"Like a lot," Lorenzo said. "Like four hundred dollars."

"Let me see what I can do."

About a week later, Fredi told Lorenzo not to worry about the cost of the class. He and Allan would cover it.

"Take the summer class and stay here," Fredi said. Though neither teacher was rolling in cash—the average teacher's salary in the district was thirty-five thousand dollars—they didn't want to see Lorenzo go.

Lorenzo was amazed. He still counted the Big Mac that Fredi had bought him in his freshman year as one of the most generous things anybody had ever done for him. But this was an entirely new level of generosity.

"Are you sure?" Lorenzo asked.

"Yeah," Fredi said. "Where would we be without your crazy ideas?"

"WE'RE GOING TO practice until we can do this without thinking," Oscar said.

It was time to put the robot together, and once the PVC pipes were glued in place, it would be difficult, if not impossible, to make changes. They would have one chance to glue it all together, and it had to be right. Oscar wanted the process to move like a finely tuned military operation. For him, the pyramid in Atlanta was just the beginning. Over his four years in high school, he had drilled his ROTC team incessantly: pushups in unison, running in lockstep, jumping jacks together. Now he brought that training to bear on Lorenzo, Cristian, and Luis. They might not have been gung ho Special Forces candidates, but Oscar had internalized the "Be all you can be" Army motto.

Under Oscar's supervision, the team assembled the robot without glue, dry-fitting pieces together. "Let's do it again," Oscar said. "The glue dries quickly so we need to move fast."

They disassembled and rebuilt the robot repeatedly. Each time, they finished at the top, leaving enough room for the black briefcase. Initially it took about an hour, but as they practiced they got faster, until they were able to do it in twenty minutes without mistakes.

It was a bittersweet exercise. The school year was coming to an end and both Oscar and Luis would be graduating just before the competition in Santa Barbara. They knew that when they glued the robot together and completed the competition, their high school years would be over. They were getting older and needed to figure out what they would do with their lives. Luis had a green card. He could keep working as a short-order cook, but he'd been doing that for years already. He felt like his diploma should mean something.

Oscar struggled with a similar but more pronounced problem. He didn't have residency and couldn't get a normal, legal job. The best he could hope for was to parlay a day laborer job into something steadier. It was hard to imagine building a life on such a shaky foundation.

Still, just graduating was an accomplishment that meant a lot to both families. Neither Oscar's nor Luis's parents had received high school diplomas, so it was an important moment in their histories. Both teens dressed in caps and gowns and promenaded up onto the stage to accept their degrees. They posed for photos and smiled happily. Oscar's sister baked a cake. Luis's mom made *birria*, a spicy beef-and-pork stew. That was all they could afford, but everyone was pleased. The day was a sign that the boys could achieve things the previous generation had not.

With graduation behind them and the contest only a few weeks away, it was time to glue the robot together. Lorenzo arrived straight from cooking class bearing snacks. He felt obligated to bring his creations to the robotics closet, since Fredi and Allan had paid for the class, but nobody was prepared for the smell of the bloated brownish-red Polish sausage.

"What is it?" Oscar asked.

"Kielbasa," Lorenzo said proudly. "And sauerkraut."

"Cook Mexican food so we can actually eat something," Cristian said.

This time, the trash talk was friendly and Lorenzo laughed with the others. It wasn't mean-spirited. Lorenzo felt like he had a real group of friends for the first time in his life. "I'm expanding your taste buds," he told them.

Oscar took a cautious bite, and soon the sausage was gone. "It was pretty good," Oscar allowed. "But let's get going."

They had practiced assembling the plastic pipes for weeks under Oscar's supervision. Now that practice would be put to use. They laid the pieces out on a table in the robotics closet and opened a metal container of Christy's Red Hot Blue Glue. The glue didn't actually need to be heated. Oscar just dipped an applicator into the container and coated it with a blob of the unnaturally blue paste.

"Whoa," Lorenzo said, getting a whiff of the stuff. It smelled like heavy-duty paint thinner and almost immediately filled the little robotics closet with an invisible cloud of intoxicating fumes. "We're gonna get high."

They decided not to place a fan near the door. They thought it would make the glue dry faster, and they didn't want it to harden while they were in the midst of placing a pipe. As a result, the vapors in the closest got denser. The guys gathered outside in the hallway. It was hard enough to remember where each of the sixty-odd pieces fit—now they were going to have to do it stoned.

"Let's take turns," Oscar said. "Take a deep breath, glue as many pieces as you can, and then run out."

They broke into teams: Oscar and Luis went first. While Luis held the first two pieces of PVC together, Oscar swabbed on some of the blue glue. Oscar was holding his breath, but the fumes stung his eyes. Even the smallest inhalation made him dizzy. He got a few pieces set in place and then rushed out.

Luis just smiled. "I'm okay. Send Cristian in."

Cristian sprinted in with his shirt pulled up over his nose and glued more pieces, while Luis continued to hold everything together with an increasingly large grin. People generally seemed small to him. Now Cristian looked like a manic elf, scurrying around the room with glowing white pipes. Luis started chuckling as the world went blurry.

Oscar suddenly appeared and grabbed him. "Hey, you've got

to get out of here." Oscar pulled him from the room. Luis couldn't stop smiling.

"Are you okay?" Oscar asked.

"Yes" was all Luis would say.

Lorenzo zipped into the room and quickly assembled a series of pieces with Cristian. The glue dried almost immediately when two pieces of pipe were pressed together, so they had to focus. One misglued portion could compromise the entire structure. It was like doing a large jigsaw puzzle with pieces that froze in place and a lack of oxygen. After sixty seconds, Cristian started to black out. He noticed his vision tunneling and had to stumble out, gasping for air.

"Damn, that's *stinky*," Lorenzo wheezed, trailing behind Cristian.

It took almost two hours to put the whole thing together amid the overpowering stench. At the end, all four teens had to work together to fit the four legs into position. Oscar felt a wave of nausea but tried to ignore it. They lowered the black briefcase into position. It was the crowning touch, the moment when the robot was complete, but there was a problem. The three pipes leading into the case didn't line up. They angled up, as if the briefcase were much bigger, creating gaps that would flood with water, shorting the entire system and sinking the robot. It was a serious problem.

"I thought you said this would work," Cristian said to Oscar.

They had practiced everything but the briefcase placement. Oscar was upset with himself. He should have tried to fit the briefcase when they were doing the dry runs. It was a critical oversight.

"We have to start over," Cristian said.

The excitement they'd felt about building the robot disappeared. The process now felt like a defeat. They had limited options. It would be impossible to salvage the pipe they had used. If they were going to start over, they'd have to buy more pipe and try again. That was a lot of added time, energy, and expense.

"We could cut out one section," Oscar offered.

While Oscar and Cristian debated the feasibility of a surgical demolition, Lorenzo held his breath and examined the pipes around the briefcase. They weren't off by much. Maybe a little heat could solve the problem.

"What if we just bend the pipe?" Lorenzo said when he came out into the hallway.

"How?" Oscar wanted to know.

"The electric heat gun."

The electric heat gun was a sort of superpowered blow-dryer. Normally it was used to dry paint, but it got hot enough to make paint peel off a surface. Lorenzo dug it out of a cabinet in the robotics closet, plugged it in, and aimed it at one of the off-angle pipes. He flipped the switch and blasted the pipe with scorching air while Luis put pressure on it. At first nothing happened. Then the PVC weakened and started to bend.

"It's working," Lorenzo shouted.

Luis angled the pipe into position, and Lorenzo flipped off the heat gun. In a moment, the PVC hardened into place exactly where it needed to be. The problem was solved.

"That was a pretty good idea," Oscar said.

"It's okay," Lorenzo said. "You can say I'm a genius."

The boys broke into laughter.

"It needs a name," Lorenzo said.

Oscar remembered Lorenzo's choking on the glue fumes and suggested, "Why don't we call it Stinky?"

BY THE SUMMER of 2004, Tina Lowe had been working at Scuba Sciences at Seventh and Sheridan for seven years. The building contained a store that sold scuba gear and, in the back, a forty-by-twenty-four-foot saltwater swimming pool. Over the years, Lowe had seen yuppies training for dive vacations in the tropics, ocean lovers trapped in the desert, and kids from nearby Brophy, an elite private school that charged eighty-seven hundred dollars a year in tuition and offered lacrosse and ice-hockey teams. The Carl Hayden robotics team was something different.

"Thank you for allowing us to use the pool," Oscar said in a crisp, almost formal manner when the team arrived rolling Stinky on a cart.

"My pleasure," Lowe said, amazed by the unusual crew filing into her facility. Luis looked like the Incredible Hulk, Cristian resembled a Mexican Bill Gates, and Lorenzo was like a mash-up of Jon Bon Jovi and a homeless kid. Michael Hanck, the skinny white kid who had designed the pumpkin-hurling trebuchet, was there too to help pilot the robot. They were supervised by an Iranian American former running coach and a white-bearded quasi-hippie. She'd never seen such a strange group walk into her scuba school.

It took them about an hour to lay out their gear. They had two battered cathode-ray-tube monitors scavenged from a dusty school district storeroom and four videogame joysticks from Radio Shack. They attached the tether, connecting the monitors to the robot's electronics. When they plugged everything in and turned the power on, the monitors filled with warbly images from the robot's twenty-seven-dollar black-and-white cameras. They jiggled the joysticks, and the propellers made a nice whirring noise. Stinky was coming to life.

Cristian was in charge of the joystick that controlled up and down movements. Hanck had the two joysticks that moved the robot forward, backward, left, and right, but the team hadn't seen much of him recently. He had struggled in school and had to enroll in summer classes. Fredi and Allan had told him that he couldn't be on the team if he dropped below a B average in his classes. As Lorenzo could attest, the rules applied to everyone.

Lorenzo manned the sensor controls. He liked to pretend he was activating the hydraulics on a tricked-out low-rider when he "hit the switches." He was responsible for the claw, the cameras, and his water-sampling pump. He did a final check on the instrumentation and gave a thumbs-up: "I'm good."

"Don't grab the pipes leading into the briefcase," Oscar warned Luis. He was worried that any pressure could create a leak. The robot resembled a twisted knot of white pipes, so it was hard to see which tube led where. Luis gingerly dipped his thick hands into the guts of the machine and hefted Stinky into the air. Oscar pulled his shirt off and slipped into the water. Stinky touched the water for the first time and drifted on the surface. It floated nicely.

"Stinky's baptized!" Lorenzo shouted.

Oscar grabbed hold of the robot and pulled down, but it wouldn't sink. It just bobbed around like a cork. Luis tried shoving down from the edge; Stinky refused to sink. It was as if it didn't want to be an underwater robot.

There was too much air inside Stinky's pipes. The team had tied on a couple of capped pipes to provide extra buoyancy, but they clearly didn't need the extra lift, so they removed one. Stinky still floated. They took off the second pipe and Stinky plummeted to the bottom of the pool. Lorenzo found a narrower piece of

PVC, capped the ends so that air was trapped inside, and affixed that to the robot. It worked: Stinky became neutrally buoyant, hovering at whatever depth it was placed at.

Their buoyancy problems weren't over though. Stinky hovered, but it tilted forward like someone leaning into a headwind. Activating the propellers would zoom it deeper. They needed something to lift Stinky's nose up.

Lorenzo pulled an empty bottle of St. Ives sunscreen out of a trash can by the pool. "What about this?"

"Garbage?" Oscar asked.

"It's got air inside."

"True." Oscar shrugged. They weren't going for style points.

Lorenzo zip tied the sunscreen bottle to the front of the robot and they lowered Stinky back into the water. This time, Stinky hovered perfectly upright. Oscar grabbed a Hula-Hoop that was leaning against a wall beside the pool. Scuba students learned to swim through them. Now it was Stinky's turn.

"See if you can drive through it," Oscar told Cristian and Hanck.

Hanck pressed forward on the controls while Cristian made Stinky dive. The robot zoomed forward, speeding through the hoops at high speed. They watched it zip through the circle on the monitors.

"That was badass," Lorenzo muttered beside them.

Cristian and Hanck stayed focused. The robot's tether was now threaded through the hoop. They turned the robot around and tried to go back through in order to pull the tether out. It was hard to drive though. Cristian tried to move the robot up in the water, but Stinky began to spin erratically. Hanck tried to steer to the left and the robot turned suddenly toward the wall of the pool.

"Watch out!" Oscar shouted.

Stinky slammed into the wall with a resounding thud.

"Can't you see where you're going?" Fredi shouted.

"Not really," Cristian explained. The walls of the pool were white and hard to make out via the video feed.

"If you hit too hard, you'll crack the PVC," Fredi told the students. "You've got to be more careful."

Cristian and Hanck tried piloting the ROV through the hoop again. Just before they reached it, the robot veered off as if it had a mind of its own and collided with the wall a second time. Stinky floated to the surface. Its electronics stopped responding.

"This is good, this is good," Oscar said, buying himself a few seconds to come up with a positive spin. They had only two weeks until the competition and he wanted everyone energized. "Did you see how hard it hit the wall? This thing's got power. Once we figure out how to drive it, we'll be the fastest team there."

BACK IN THE ROBOTICS CLOSET, Cristian reexamined every single connection inside the briefcase. Some of the short PWM cables connecting the joystick to the ROV controller had been damaged and caused the robot to behave erratically during its pool test. They had gotten the wires off the robot they'd taken to Atlanta and repurposed them for Stinky. That saved some money but also meant they were dealing with recycled cables. The only other PWM wires they had were eight feet long. It wasn't ideal—the unneeded length would clutter the cramped briefcase—but it was the best they could do. Cristian coiled the long wire inside the case and made the connections. When he powered the system on again, the joysticks seemed to work fine.

"We also need to change the acceleration curve," Cristian said. The slightest touch on the joystick sent Stinky flying. That needed to be corrected, so Cristian worked with Allan to reprogram the ROV's software.

Lorenzo couldn't program, but he knew for sure that the robot was aesthetically challenged. The blue glue had dripped down the joints, leaving messy blue streaks across the robot's white plastic framing. It looked as if the machine were bleeding blue blood from every orifice.

"This robot is ugly as hell," he concluded.

Lorenzo decided to solve two problems at once by giving Stinky a makeover. He pulled red, blue, and yellow paint out of a cupboard in the robotics closet and set to work. He applied red paint to any section that Luis should avoid grabbing: the tubes leading into the briefcase and the delicate camera housings. He painted the ROV's corners yellow so they could better see the outline of the robot underwater. He colored the rest blue and told Luis to only grab the blue parts.

"Okay," Luis said simply.

A week later, they returned to Scuba Sciences. The competition was seven days away. Lowe was accustomed to teenage boys who talked about chasing girls and playing video games. These kids were fully focused on their robot. The lingo—acceleration curves and pulse-width modulation—sounded like a foreign language.

"What's your girlfriend think about this?" she asked Oscar.

Oscar looked at his feet. "I don't have a girlfriend."

"Good," Lowe said. "This is more important for you right now."

"Yes, ma'am," Oscar said, trying not to blush.

In comparison to their first pool test, this second session was a success. Cristian and Hanck steered clear of the walls, and Stinky responded better to the joystick. The robot also took accurate depth measurements, the mechanical claw retrieved a piece of PVC pipe, and they deployed the tape measure. Oscar put together a list of all the tasks and ranked them based on importance and feasibility. The easiest ones with the highest points would get done first. He got a clipboard and barked orders like the captain of a ship.

After watching the team practice all the maneuvers they would have to do in the contest, Oscar placed Lorenzo's liquid sampling at the bottom of his feasibility list. The small, copper suction pipe was too hard to position. During the competition, they would have to insert the pipe into a half-inch hole. They tried practicing with a piece of three-quarter-inch PVC tube, but they couldn't get the copper pipe into the larger-diameter hole. The pump system functioned, however, and could suck up five hundred milliliters of water in twenty seconds. Stinky just couldn't make precise movements. That task seemed hopeless.

It didn't really matter though. Stinky zipped around the pool with ease. Fredi got in the pool, grabbed on to the robot, and got dragged through the water. The trolling motors were small but powerful. Hanck and Cristian worked well together, and over their two sessions driving the robot, they learned how to steer in tandem. They were all starting to feel a touch of confidence.

So it was a shock when, the day before their departure, Fredi and Allan announced that Hanck wouldn't be coming to Santa Barbara. They had told him he needed at least a B in summer school to travel to Santa Barbara, and he had slipped below that. As a result, he wouldn't be allowed to compete. The team had less than twenty-four hours until their departure, and they had just lost one of their two drivers.

They were gathered around the narrow table in the robotics closet. The fumes had dissipated so it wasn't toxic to hang out in the room anymore, but the mood was grim. Cristian couldn't drive the robot by himself because there were three joysticks. He didn't have enough hands. Lorenzo had already figured out how to operate all the sensors, and Luis was needed by the edge of the pool to manage the tether and lift the robot. There was only one choice.

"I'll figure it out and we'll be fine," Oscar said. He sounded confident, but he knew it was a setback.

Fredi called Lowe and asked if the pool was available for another practice session. Classes were booked, but she agreed to give them as much time as she could between sessions. They packed up Stinky, raced over to Seventh Avenue, and started setting up while scuba-diving students emerged dripping from the pool and plodded past.

"Okay, you've got forty-five minutes till the next class," Lowe told them.

Luis lowered Stinky into the water, and Oscar grabbed the two joysticks that controlled the robot's horizontal movements. "Since we changed the acceleration algorithm, you can push the joystick forward a bit and it won't take off," Cristian coached him. Oscar tapped the joystick, and Stinky responded by cruising forward into a wall. They could hear the deep thud of the impact.

"Slow down," Cristian said worriedly.

Oscar eased Stinky forward while Cristian pressed his joystick forward, causing the robot to descend. "Let's try tilting forward," Cristian said. To pick up objects, they had to be able to tilt and inch forward. Cristian gave the robot a quick hit of upward acceleration, tilting the whole bot forward. Oscar juiced the controls but gave it too much power. Stinky nearly did a somersault.

"That's too much," Cristian chided.

"I know," Oscar snapped. It wasn't easy.

"Let's just try cruising around."

They did a number of laps around the pool, and Oscar was able to avoid the walls. Right when he felt he might be getting the hang of it, Lowe walked out into the pool area. "I'm afraid that's all the time I can give you."

THE TEAM MEMBERS were due to gather at the Carl Hayden parking lot at 4:00 a.m. on Thursday, June 24, 2004. It was dark out when everyone arrived, and the roads were nearly empty. Allan and Fredi unlocked the Marine Science building while Oscar, Luis, and Cristian waited. Oscar looked at his watch. It was four and Lorenzo wasn't there.

In the eight months since Lorenzo had missed the pumpkin-hurling event, he'd become surprisingly dependable. If the team had a meeting after school, he was always there. When Fredi told him he had to improve his grades, he studied hard and managed to raise his geometry grade from an F to a B+. He had sworn that he'd never be late again, and the team now trusted him. They couldn't do this without him, so his absence now worried everybody.

"There he is," Oscar said with relief as Lorenzo jogged up.

"You can all relax because I'm here now," Lorenzo said, holding his arms up as if he were a soccer player who'd just scored a goal.

"Last thing I'm going to do is relax," Oscar said. "Particularly with you around."

They started hauling everything they would need out of the robotics closet: toolboxes, the two video monitors, and Stinky. Sam Alexander, a marine science teacher at Carl Hayden, pitched in. He was coming along to help chaperone. They loaded up a cart and rolled the heavy stuff to the school van, a beige 1993 Ford Econoline. Stinky wasn't going to be traveling in style. They hefted the robot into the back and slammed the door.

Oscar and Luis piled into the cramped cab of Fredi's 1989 Silverado truck. Since they had graduated, they couldn't ride in a school vehicle, which was fine by them. The van was jammed with equipment, and they were happy to miss Lorenzo's running commentary on everything he saw out the window.

Unfortunately, Allan had provided each vehicle with a portable ham radio and taught Lorenzo how to operate it. "Wassup wassup?" Lorenzo's voice crackled over the radio as they got onto Interstate 10 and headed west. Oscar groaned.

Allan told Lorenzo to keep it to essential communications. They had a seven-hour drive ahead of them and needed to conserve the batteries. Plus, their time would be better spent reviewing their engineering presentation. Nearly half of the points in the contest were based on how well they were able to defend their ideas in front of a panel of professional engineers and ROV experts from NASA and the Navy. Each of them had to be ready to answer any question.

"What's a PWM cable?" Allan asked.

"PWM," Lorenzo replied automatically. "Pulse-width modulation. *Esto* controls analog circuits with digital output."

"You think Luis has it down?" Allan asked. Luis rarely said much of anything, so it was hard to tell what he knew.

"That's an essential communication," Lorenzo said, picking up the radio and depressing the talk button. "Wassup, wassup?"

"Can you be serious?" Cristian demanded.

"I am serious." Lorenzo fired off, "Yo, Luis, what's the index of refraction?"

Oscar and Luis looked at each other in Fredi's car. "Do you know it?" Oscar asked.

"Uhhh . . ." Luis wasn't totally sure, but he thought he knew. In a moment, Lorenzo's radio rumbled with Luis's voice:

"It's about light and water. About how fast light goes through water."

"That's right," Cristian said. "Ask him what the number is."

Lorenzo radioed the request. Luis didn't know, so they started drilling each other over the radio. The Sonoran Desert airwaves filled with questions about spike relays, underwater-camera housings, and transmitter frequencies. They went back and forth until they crossed the California border. Outside, in the fields around the town of Blythe, laborers picked watermelons in the hundred-degree heat.

Lorenzo fell silent. His family was still struggling to avoid eviction. The Realtor they had appealed to for help had paid off their overdue mortgage payments in exchange for the deed to the property. They were now renting the house back from the guy, but it was a precarious situation. It seemed they may have only gotten into more trouble. Lorenzo worried that he could come home to find out he was homeless. There was a real chance that he'd end up picking in the fields like the people he was looking at now. This four-day trip could be his last chance to experience what it felt like to do something other than manual labor.

THREE

THE TEAM ROLLED into Santa Barbara in the afternoon and wended their way onto the UCSB campus. A low-hanging cloud layer had built up on the ocean and drifted over the area, covering the school in a blanket of gray. It was classic June gloom, a late-spring, early-summer Southern California phenomenon. The overcast skies didn't bother Lorenzo. He caught intermittent glimpses of the Pacific and was enthralled. It was the first time he'd seen the ocean.

"It's incredifying," he said, meaning it was both incredible and terrifying.

They unloaded everything into the dorm room they had been assigned and spent the night making sure that everything still worked. At first, it didn't. They pushed one of the beds onto its side and planted Stinky on the floor. When they turned the power on, the thrusters refused to reverse. Then, when they let go of the joysticks, the robot whirred into action. It seemed as if a ghost were operating it.

"It's got voodoo," Lorenzo said.

It was the last thing they needed on the eve of the competition: a robot that wouldn't even respond to their commands. But after an hour, the controls mysteriously started working again. It was as if the desert heat they'd driven through had tweaked Stinky's brain. They were relieved that they didn't have to dismantle, diagnose, and rebuild the robot. It had been a long day of travel, and this last scare made them feel a little tweaked too. The ocean was within walking distance. There were beautiful beaches to explore, but they all went to sleep early.

Around nine the next morning, the Carl Hayden team rolled Stinky into a UCSB pool reserved for practice. Other teams were scattered around the perimeter and glanced at the newcomers. The robots on display looked like works of art to the Carl Hayden kids. The competitors appeared to have all the things they didn't: glass syntactic foam, machined metal, elaborate control panels, and cool matching outfits. Cristian was proud of his robot, but he could see that it looked like a Geo Metro compared with the Lexuses and BMWs around the pool. He had thought that Lorenzo's paint job was nice. Now it just looked clownish.

Despite appearances, the other teams had struggled to build robots capable of completing the mission. MIT fielded a team of twelve undergraduates and had landed a ten-thousand-dollar grant from ExxonMobil, the world's largest corporation at the time. The team was comprised of seven ocean-engineering majors, three mechanical-engineering students, and two computer science majors. But two weeks before the competition, their control system had overheated and melted, emitting a plume of blue smoke. Thaddeus Stefanov-Wagner, a team member who had competed in the 2003 MATE event as a high schooler, scrambled to rebuild the controls and managed to do it in a week.

MIT's problems didn't end there: their ROV was damaged during shipping. It arrived in Santa Barbara in a wooden crate that had been partially crushed. But within minutes of its removal from the box, everybody on the team had their hands on it, each addressing their area of responsibility. For sophomore Jordan Stanway, the team leader, it was the best moment of the entire school year: a highly trained, highly functioning team working in perfect coordination. He had come to MIT to study ocean engineering and was proud to be part of a team as skilled as this one.

The boys from Carl Hayden shuffled to an unclaimed portion of pool perimeter. "Damn," Lorenzo muttered as he caught a glimpse of the MIT team. Their robot featured a large EXXON-MOBIL sticker and was the smallest, most densely instrumented robot at the competition. The group wore matching blue shirts emblazoned with the words MIT ROV TEAM. They were white and most had brownish-blond hair.

To Lorenzo, they looked like the embodiment of power. "I've never seen so many white people in one place," he marveled.

"Let's focus," Oscar ordered. They were scheduled to appear for their engineering review that afternoon, which meant they only had a few hours to practice in the pool. Every second counted now.

Luis gently lowered Stinky into the water and grunted that the robot was ready. Oscar and Cristian motored Stinky forward and down, but the robot started turning.

"Go straight," Fredi shouted.

"I am going straight," Oscar responded.

"No, you're not, you're going left," Fredi said.

"Let me try," Cristian said, taking the horizontal controls from Oscar. He tried to get the robot to bank right, but it wasn't working. "Pull it out!" Cristian shouted to Luis.

Luis speedily pulled Stinky to the surface and lifted the robot out of the water. Fredi, Allan, and the kids gathered around the dripping, brightly colored frame. Lorenzo opened the briefcase top and looked inside.

"It's got to be the programming," Fredi said.

"It's not the programming," Allan snapped.

"It's the water," Lorenzo said. Everybody looked at him. "There's water inside the briefcase." He pointed, and the others could see a tablespoon of water on the bottom of the briefcase.

"Why didn't it just short out?" Cristian asked.

He gently tapped the PWM wires connecting the joysticks to the control board. The robot's propellers whirred to life. At first, it seemed like good news. The robot was still working. In reality, it meant they had two problems: the cables needed to be resoldered and there was a leak.

BACK IN THEIR dorm room, Fredi and Allan were worried. The robot wasn't working, and the kids were scheduled to go in front of the NASA and Navy experts within hours. Stinky was turning out to be a failure from the outset. The kids felt defeated before the competition had even begun.

Oscar wasn't ready to give up. "Let's take it apart now," he argued. "We can fix it."

Fredi didn't want the kids preoccupied when they presented themselves to the experts. They had to be mentally ready for what would likely be an intense grilling. "Look, don't worry about the robot right now," he said. "We've got all night to fix it."

"It's more important to get ready for the review," Allan said. The kids had limited experience talking in front of imposing professionals. Raising money and competing in the FIRST program had helped, but talking to an audience was still a novel experience. That, coupled with their shaken confidence, could undermine everything they'd accomplished so far. They might leave Santa Barbara convinced that the whole thing was a mistake, that it wasn't their lot to be ambitious.

They needed to be jolted into a better frame of mind, so Allan decided on a gamble. "Everybody come with me," he commanded.

The team followed him out of the dorm to a bridge. Though it was summertime, there was still a steady flow of pedestrians.

"I want you guys to hang out here and talk to anybody who comes by," Allan said.

"What do you want us to talk about?" Oscar asked.

"Say, 'Hi, would you like to hear about our thrusters?'" Allan prompted.

Lorenzo snickered. "I don't think nobody is going to talk to us if we say that."

"Tell them you built a robot," Allan persevered. "They'll want to hear about it."

Fredi and Allan walked off and watched from a distance. The locals might ignore the kids or think that they were panhandling. That could further undermine their already fragile state of mind. Allan was hoping that wouldn't happen. He was banking on the kindness of strangers.

The kids were bashful at first and let a handful of people walk by. Oscar gripped a white, plastic, three-ring binder that contained drawings of Stinky's innovations.

Finally Lorenzo mustered up the courage to talk to a man who looked like a professor. "Hi, we're high school students from Phoenix, and we're here to compete in an underwater-robotics contest. Do you want to hear about it?"

The man laughed. "Okay. What does your robot do?"

Oscar stepped forward with his three-ring binder and flipped to the first page, which displayed a photo of Stinky. "It's an ROV. That means 'remotely operated vehicle.'" He explained that Stinky was designed to retrieve underwater objects, record video, sample fluid, measure distances, and locate sounds.

"It can do all that?" the man said.

"When it's working, yeah," Oscar said. "Right now it's kind of messed up."

"Well, I'll be rooting for you," the man said, and, after wishing them luck, headed away.

After that, the team stopped a variety of people and explained why their robot was so cool, even if it was on life support. Cristian talked about applying the index of refraction to their laser range findings, and Lorenzo bragged about his "ghetto" liquid sampling tool. The people they talked to seemed impressed by the ragtag group of teens, and the reaction they got gave them a boost. It reminded them that they were doing something they had never done before. In Phoenix, they were called illegal aliens and pegged as criminals. They were alternately viewed as American, Mexican, or neither. Now, for a moment, they were simply teenagers at a robotics competition by the ocean.

IN THE HALLWAY outside the review room, Allan and Fredi waited anxiously for the kids. They knew that the panel was comprised of some impressive judges. There was Tom Swean, the gruff fifty-eight-year-old who ran the Navy's Ocean Engineering and Marine Systems program. Lisa Spence, the flight lead at NASA's Neutral Buoyancy Laboratory, was also in there grilling the kids. Teachers had the option of joining in the review, but Allan and Fredi decided to let their kids go solo. It was a vote of confidence, but it also meant the two teachers had nothing to do but worry.

"How do you think they're doing?" Allan asked.

"The other teams were in for at least forty-five minutes," Fredi said. "If they come out before then, I think it's a bad sign."

After twenty-five minutes, the door opened and the Carl Hayden kids streamed out. Allan glanced at Fredi. It was a bad sign.

"How'd you do, guys?" Allan said enthusiastically, trying to mask his disappointment.

"We did great!" Oscar enthused.

Allan thought the kids might be shaken, but all four were smiling. They were convinced that they had answered the judges' questions perfectly. It was obvious to Allan and Fredi that the kids were overconfident. They couldn't have done that well.

Either way, it was over. Now the team had to repair their robot before its scheduled competition in the morning. They had less than twenty-four hours to fix both the leak and the loose wiring. Allan knew exactly what they needed to do first: go to Sizzler. Nobody was going to solve anything on an empty stomach.

On the short van ride to the restaurant, Oscar led a brainstorming session: "There's no way we can buy a new briefcase and get everything rewired in time. We need to come up with something quick and easy."

"You need a desiccant," Fredi said. "Something that will soak up the moisture."

"But it's got to fit inside the case," Cristian pointed out. "It's got to be small and superabsorbent."

An image from television flashed through Lorenzo's mind. "Absorbent? Like a tampon?"

Oscar, Cristian, and Luis laughed. It sounded ridiculous to them.

"Actually, that's a perfect idea," Fredi said.

After ordering the all-you-can-eat dinner and downing more shrimp than he'd consumed in his life, Lorenzo found himself standing in the parking lot of a Ralphs grocery store near the UCSB campus. Behind him, in the van, his teammates egged him on.

"Go on," Oscar said. "It was your idea."

"So why do I have to get them? Somebody else should have to."

"Go," Oscar ordered.

"I don't know which ones to get."

"So ask someone."

Lorenzo headed for the store. It was done up to look like a hacienda, complete with a red-tile roof, white walls, and freshly planted palms. He walked inside and wandered past the organic-produce section, trying to build up his courage. He passed an elderly lady examining eggplant—he was too embarrassed to ask her. Next, he saw a young woman in jeans shopping for shampoo.

"Excuse me, madam." He wasn't used to approaching women by himself, let alone well-dressed white women. He saw apprehension flash across her face. Maybe she thought he was trying to sell magazines or candy bars, but he steeled himself. He explained that he was building a robot for an underwater contest sponsored by NASA, and his robot was leaking. He wanted to soak up the water with tampons but didn't know which ones to buy. "Could you help me buy the most best tampons?"

The woman broke into a big smile and led him to feminine hygiene. She handed him a box of o.b. ultra-absorbency. "These don't have an applicator, so they'll be easier to fit inside your robot."

He stared at the ground, mumbled his thanks, and headed quickly for the checkout.

"I hope you win," she called out, laughing.

THEY GOT BACK to the dorm room and circled up around Stinky. A bunch of the joystick wires were clearly disconnected from the controller, and there was no way to simply resolder the few that had popped loose. They had to pull all sixty-four wires and start over. It would take hours and they were already tired from the tension of the morning's failed practice session and the engineering review. Plus, they were full of steak and shrimp. Everybody just wanted to go to sleep, but they had only until dawn to get the robot working.

"I'll stay up and do it," Oscar volunteered.

"I'll do it with you," Lorenzo offered.

Over the past nine months, Oscar hadn't taken Lorenzo seriously. Oscar judged others by his own level of commitment, and Lorenzo always seemed to come up short. Lorenzo cracked jokes and spouted strange (though often innovative) ideas. Throughout the year, Oscar had been half prepared for Lorenzo to drop off the team and never show up again. But in this moment, Oscar realized that Lorenzo was intensely committed. Good engineering solutions had value. But, to Oscar, doing things that no one else wanted to do, toughing it out and being a soldier, that's what counted. For the first time, he felt real respect for his teammate.

"All right, let's do it," Oscar said.

Luis and Cristian went to sleep in another room. Allan took a bed in the corner, and Fredi fell asleep on the floor with all the lights on. Stinky sat where the other bed used to be—the teens had flipped it up and propped it against the wall. Oscar and Lorenzo hunched over the electronics on the carpet. Sixty-four wires the size of a single hair needed to be meticulously fitted into individual, small holes and then topped with a dash of solder.

Lorenzo positioned the wires in the holes, while Oscar melted the solder with the soldering iron. With each drop of solder, a small puff of gray smoke trellised into the air. They barely talked during the delicate, nerve-racking work. If Oscar hit the wire with the soldering iron, the wire would instantly melt and disappear, forcing them to pull out everything they'd done, restrip all the wires, and start over.

By the time they had done fifty wires, it was roughly two in the morning. Their eyes hurt after hours of staring at tiny wires. The stakes were higher now too. A mistake now would mean ripping out the completed connections. If that happened, they wouldn't have enough time to resolder everything before the competition. Every connection needed to be perfect now.

"Let's take a break for a second," Oscar said.

They sat back and rubbed their eyes. The room was filled with an acrid, burnt smell. Everybody else was asleep.

"Thanks for staying up with me," Oscar said.

"You think I'm going let you do this by yourself?" Lorenzo said. Oscar thought Lorenzo meant that they were all in this together until Lorenzo added, "You'd probably screw it up if I wasn't watching you."

Lorenzo grinned at him with a big, crooked-tooth goofy smile. Oscar chuckled. He never would have been friends with a kid like Lorenzo, but now he was glad they were teammates.

"Shut up," Oscar said, picking up the solder gun. "Let's get this done." They had fourteen left. Oscar moved carefully and slowly while Lorenzo positioned the fifty-first wire.

Lorenzo said a silent prayer to the Virgin Mary, and they worked through the final batch of wires, connecting the last one around 2:30 a.m. They turned the power on and tested the joysticks. The machine worked.

THE BANNER ABOVE the pool declared WELCOME TO THE 2004 NATIONAL ROV COMPETITION. A set of high-powered fans blew across the surface, obscuring the view below. Teams could make out the vague outline of a large black structure but nothing more. A loudspeaker blared Hawaiian music. This was the main event: the underwater portion of the Explorer-class competition had begun.

Monterey Peninsula College was called to the pool. Their fifteen-person team deployed three vehicles: two ROVs—dubbed Romulus and Remus—and a third craft, the Sea Wolf, which served as their eyes in the sky. It floated on the surface with a camera system to guide the operation. Romulus was a heavy-lift submersible and ran off three car batteries in the command tent. Remus was a smaller, more agile bot designed to explore the interior of the mocked-up submarine. Even with all that robotic firepower, Monterey only picked up 30 out of 110 points. The mission tasks were proving to be even more difficult than anticipated.

Cape Fear Community College managed a slightly more successful run. Their robot had a beautiful extruded-aluminum frame with a shiny blue fiberglass-covered foam top. They called it the Sea Devil 3. Its shell gleamed so nicely in the morning sun that Allan took to calling the bot a piece of "underwater jewelry." One of its most impressive features was a chamber at the top that was connected to a scuba tank in the command tent. It allowed the operators to add to or remove air from the chamber to fine-tune buoyancy on the fly. When the robot picked up a heavy object and had trouble surfacing, they sent a blast of air down a tube and the ROV came right up. It was a good idea with solid engineering behind it, and yet they managed to post only 40 points by the end of their thirty-minute run.

There were eleven teams in the Explorer division, and all of them had chosen to measure themselves against a higher standard. As a result, most of the teams were more confident and accomplished, and all of them posted at least 5 points. Nonetheless, some experienced catastrophic failures early in their missions. Their robots simply sank to the bottom of the pool and sat there, unresponsive. After a few minutes of fruitless troubleshooting, the teams had to ignominiously haul their robots out of the water by the tether. One stranded robot emitted a giant air bubble from the depths.

Lorenzo watched from the side of the pool and laughed. "It farted."

Lorenzo's joking didn't lighten the mood. If these other teams were struggling, it meant that Carl Hayden should expect to have an even tougher time. The Explorer division was clearly punishingly difficult, but it also gave them a sliver of hope. If they could just get their robot to work and complete a single task, they'd be ahead of the teams whose robots shorted out. That meant they wouldn't finish last.

The judges called MIT to the pool, and the college students lowered their compact, welded-aluminum ROV into the water. They quickly piled up points. They sped around the pool, locating objects and confidently investigating the interior of the mocked-up submarine. Locating the underwater pinger was one of the most challenging tasks. The event organizers had scattered four dummy pingers around the pool so that teams wouldn't luck into picking the right one. MIT located it using their Knowles Acoustics MR-8406 underwater microphone.

They weren't perfect though. They found the barrel with the leaking fluid and maneuvered up to it. This task was worth

15 points—more than any other. Since 3 points were subtracted for diluting the red sample fluid with pool water, the MIT team built a dual bladder system. When their pump was activated, it would fill one bladder and then a second. In theory, the pool water already in their sampling tube would flow into the first bladder, before the second bladder filled with unadulterated red fluid. The only problem: they couldn't get their sampling tube into the barrel. The opening was too narrow. MIT gave up and sped away, confirming what Oscar had suspected: the task was impossible. Still, MIT had amassed 48 points, putting them in first place.

On the edge of the pool, Lorenzo was cramming tampons around Stinky's circuit board, lining the edges with clumps of the cottony things. He and Oscar were operating on a few hours of sleep, but they were amped up.

"Put one over there," Oscar ordered, pointing to a corner of the briefcase.

"I know what I'm doing," Lorenzo said, ignoring Oscar. He felt that the tampons were his domain. He'd earned the right to put them wherever he wanted.

"We need Carl Hayden High School on deck," one of the judges said over the PA system.

Their time had come.

"Okay, guys," Allan told the kids. "You probably won't have more than ten minutes before the leak shorts the controls, so go as fast as you can for the easy stuff."

"Just get some points," Fredi said. "That'll put you ahead of a lot of teams."

"We will," Oscar said confidently.

The teachers watched the boys roll their equipment toward the "command shack," a somewhat flimsy aluminum structure draped with a large, blue plastic tarp. It created a tented shelter that was enclosed on three sides.

"Boy, I hope this works," Allan said.

"Me too," Fredi responded.

The judges started a timer. Like the other contestants, Carl Hayden had five minutes to set up inside the shack and complete a safety check. Everybody burst into action. Oscar and Lorenzo rolled their monitor cart into position inside the darkened structure. Cristian carried a piece of particleboard that held the joysticks and topside electronics. Luis off-loaded Stinky onto the edge of the pool and handed the tether to Cristian, who connected it to the control system. Lorenzo fitted a purple balloon onto Stinky's bilge pump. Oscar flipped the power switch.

Stinky was operational.

Leah Herbert checked a box on the score sheet beside the words *Team is ready for the mission.* Herbert was an ROV specialist at Oceaneering International, a company that builds and operates ROVs primarily for the oil and gas industry. She was flanked by judges Bryan Schaefer and William Kirkwood, two ROV specialists from the Monterey Bay Aquarium Research Institute. Together, they would determine which tasks had been completed and award points accordingly.

"You guys are clear to get wet," Herbert told them. "You've got thirty minutes."

"Okay, Luis, let's go," Oscar said.

Luis lowered Stinky into the water, and Lorenzo prayed again to the Virgin Mary. He prayed that the tampons would work, but then wondered if the Virgin got her period and whether it was appropriate for him to be praying to her about tampons. He tried to think of a different saint to pray to but couldn't come up with a good one. The whir of propellers brought him back to the competition.

Stinky careened wildly as it dived toward the bottom. Luis stood at the pool's edge, paying out the tether cable. From the control tent, Cristian, Oscar, and Lorenzo monitored Stinky's descent on their videoscreens. Via the robot's front-facing camera, they could see the bright, sparkling poolscape that Stinky was moving through.

"There's something there." Cristian pointed. Down below, they could see a black object on an elevated tarp. It was the towfish, a mock-up of an underwater sonar device. Just seeing it was worth 5 points. The judges standing behind them in the command shack made a notation. With 5 points, they were tied for last place.

"*Vámonos*, Cristian, this is it!" Oscar said, pushing his controls too far forward. They were nervous and overcompensated for each other's joystick movements, causing Stinky to veer off course. The towfish and tarp disappeared off their screens.

"Go back!" Cristian said.

"I got it." Oscar corrected course and they sped down toward the object.

"You're going too fast," Cristian said.

Oscar hit reverse, and the propeller blast pushed the towfish off the tarp. They circled the tarp but could no longer reach the towfish.

"Let's do the next thing," Oscar said hurriedly. He didn't want to waste any time.

"What's that?" Lorenzo asked, pointing to an object on the screen. It looked like a barrel.

"It's the fluid-sampling thing," Cristian said.

"That's last," Oscar said. "Let's keep moving."

They rotated and saw the looming mass of the mocked-up submarine in the distance. So far, Stinky was holding up. The joysticks were functioning and the robot responded to all their commands. Oscar pushed forward and Stinky motored toward the structure. Cristian pulled back, and Stinky moved toward the surface.

"Let's try to do the measuring," Oscar said.

They managed to hook the loop of their tape measure onto the end of the submarine and reversed, spooling the tape out. When they reached the end of the sub, Lorenzo flicked on the black-and-white camera that was pointed at the tape measure. The screen was pure white.

"I can't see anything," Oscar said.

The camera exposure had been set when they were indoors at Scuba Sciences. During their practice run the previous day, it had been hazy in Santa Barbara. Now the sun was shining strongly, and the light overwhelmed the iris. The measurement was there—they just couldn't see it.

Still, they got 5 points for deploying the tape measure. They motored over to the sub's "periscope"—a tall plastic tube—and aimed their laser range finder at the bottom. Again, it gave a reading, but the image coming from the camera was blown out and they couldn't see it. They got 5 points for being able to hover beside the periscope while gauging the depth even if they couldn't actually report the measurement.

Most of the remaining tasks involved entering the submarine structure, a hazardous endeavor. Oscar was worried that Stinky could get snagged, ending their mission.

He checked the time: they had fifteen minutes left. "Let's go back to the barrel.".

"I thought we were going to do that last," Cristian said.

"Let's just try it." Oscar spun the robot and headed back toward the barrel.

At Scuba Sciences, they usually couldn't place Stinky's bent copper proboscis into a half-inch pipe. The few times they did, it took dozens of tries over hours. Now the minutes were counting down on their mission. Cristian wasn't sure it was worth trying, but Oscar was in charge.

The teens readjusted their grips on the joysticks and leaned into the monitors as Stinky approached the barrel that had frustrated the MIT team. The "barrel" was a one-gallon paint can painted with red and green camouflage. A half-inch tube protruded five and a half inches out the top. The control tent was silent. Now that they were focused on the mission, both Oscar and Cristian relaxed and made almost imperceptibly small movements with their joysticks. Oscar tapped his control forward, while Cristian gave a short backward blast on the vertical propellers. As Stinky floated forward a half inch, its rear raised up and the sampling pipe sank perfectly into the drum.

"*Dios mío*," Oscar whispered, not fully believing what he saw.

"Hit the switches," Cristian shrieked.

Lorenzo had already activated the pump and was counting out twenty seconds in a decidedly unscientific way.

"*Uno, dos, tres, cuatro . . . ,*" he mumbled, until he got to twenty. He turned the pump off. They couldn't see if the balloon had filled, so there was no telling if it had worked.

"Let's get it to Luis," Oscar said.

Oscar backed Stinky out of the barrel. They spun the robot around and piloted it back to Luis at the edge of the pool. He hauled Stinky out of the water, and Oscar, Cristian, and Lorenzo poured out of the command shack. The purple balloon sat plumply inside Lorenzo's hacked-open milk container.

Oscar carefully removed the balloon. Cristian grabbed a plastic graduated cylinder to measure the fluid inside. Finding the barrel was worth 5 points. Collecting a sample and returning it to the control shack was worth another 5. They'd get 1 additional point for every hundred milliliters they collected—up to five hundred milliliters, for a total of 5 possible extra points. Oscar began to pour the liquid into the cylinder.

"*Ciento, doscientos, trescientos*," Cristian said with mounting excitement as Oscar poured the fluid in. Finally: *quinientos*—five hundred milliliters. They had collected a complete, though slightly diluted, sample and would receive a wholloping 12 points. That brought them to 27 points so far, more than most of the other teams.

"Can we make a little noise?" Cristian asked Pat Barrow, a NASA lab operations manager supervising the contest.

"Go on ahead," he replied.

Cristian started yelling. Luis stood there with a silly grin on his face, while his friends danced around him. They had done something that some of the best engineering students in the country had failed to accomplish.

"Let's go, let's go," Oscar said, cutting the celebration short. They still had ten minutes left and he didn't want to waste any more time. They were now in contention for a top spot. Luis quickly lowered the ROV back into the water.

Oscar piloted Stinky toward the submarine. They hadn't yet explored the interior and there were a lot more points to be won. Cristian kept Stinky level as Oscar motored gingerly forward. The robot inched into the structure, trailing its tether. The walls were black and the passageway was treacherously narrow. The tether began to grind against the structure, pulling them back. Seconds ticked away and they weren't getting anywhere.

"We've got to do something different," Oscar said.

With a minute left, Oscar tried to make a tight turn, and the prop wash blew open a compartment, revealing a golden bell.

"That's the captain's bell," Cristian shouted.

As the time ran out on their mission, the judges marked them down for another 5 points. That meant they had amassed 32 points. Not only had they not finished last, their mission score placed them in third place behind MIT and Cape Fear Community College. Everything would be determined now by the scores they received on their engineering review.

Fredi and Allan couldn't believe it. They rushed to the command shack. Fredi snapped pictures as if the kids were celebrities. Allan grabbed Cristian and shook him like a tree.

"Congratulations," Allan said. "You officially don't suck."

"Can we go to Hooters if we win?" Lorenzo asked.

"Sure," Fredi said with a laugh. "And Dr. Cameron and I will retire too."

THE AWARDS CEREMONY took place over dinner, and the Carl Hayden team was glad for that. Oscar felt as if he had run twenty miles with a fifty pound rucksack, and even flavorless iceberg lettuce looked good to him. Their nerves had calmed. Fredi and Allan tried to temper their expectations. The teens felt that they had done great during the engineering review but, in reality, they probably hadn't. The teachers told them that they had probably placed somewhere in the middle of the pack. They'd be lucky to get fourth or fifth overall. Privately, each of them was hoping they'd hold on to third. No matter what, they agreed, they were proud of what they had accomplished.

The first award was a surprise: a Special Prize that wasn't listed in the program. Bryce Merrill, the bearded, middle-aged recruiting manager for Oceaneering International, an industrial ROV design firm, was the announcer. He explained that the judges had created this spontaneously to honor special achievement. He stood behind a podium on the temporary stage and glanced down at his notes. The contestants sat crowded around a dozen tables. Carl Hayden High School, he said, was that special team.

The guys trotted up to the stage, forcing smiles. It seemed obvious that this was a condescending pat on the back, as if to say, "You did well, considering where you came from." They didn't want to be "special"—they wanted third. It signaled to them that they'd missed it.

They returned to their seats, and Fredi and Allan shook their hands.

"Good job, guys," Fredi said, trying to sound pleased. "You did well. They probably gave you that for the tampon."

"Hey, you got an award," Allan pointed out. "Everybody back home is going to be really proud of you."

Allan and Fredi tried to look on the bright side. Nobody had expected them to get *any* award. It was actually pretty amazing.

Oscar nodded. Allan was right. The whole team had come farther than even they had expected. Maybe they hadn't placed at the top of the rankings, but everybody now knew that they were talented engineers. That was a pretty remarkable accomplishment on its own.

"Come on, guys," Oscar said encouragingly. "This is great. For the rest of our lives, we can say we won an award here."

Lorenzo decided it was fun just to have gotten up onstage and have everyone clap for him. He'd remember that forever.

THE CEREMONY WAS coming to an end. A few small prizes were handed out (Terrific Tether Management, Perfect Pickup Tool), and then Merrill moved on to the final awards: Design Elegance, Technical Report, and Overall Winner. The MIT students shifted in their seats and stretched their legs. While they had been forced to skip the fluid sampling, they had completed more underwater tasks overall than any other team. The Cape Fear team had posted the second-highest number of points during the underwater mission. They sat across the room, fidgeted with their napkins, and tried not to look nervous. The students from Monterey Peninsula College looked straight ahead. They'd placed fourth behind Carl Hayden in the underwater trials. They were the most likely third-place finishers. It would all come down to how the judges graded the teams' oral and written presentations. The guys from Phoenix glanced back at the buffet table and wondered if they could get more cake before the ceremony wrapped up.

Then Merrill leaned into the microphone and said that the ROV named Stinky had captured the design award.

"What did he just say?" Lorenzo asked.

"Oh my God!" Fredi shouted. "Stand up!"

It didn't make any sense to Lorenzo. There was nothing pretty or elegant about their robot. Compared to the gleaming machines other teams had constructed, Stinky was a study in simplicity. The PVC, the balloon, the tape measure—in each case they had chosen the most straightforward solution to a problem. It was an approach that grew naturally out of watching family members fix cars, manufacture mattresses, and lay irrigation piping. To a large swath of the population, driveway mechanics, box-frame builders, and gardeners did not represent the cutting edge of engineering know-how. They were low-skilled laborers who didn't have access to real technology. Stinky represented this low-tech approach to engineering.

But that was exactly what had impressed the judges. Lisa Spence, the NASA judge, believed that there was no reason to come up with a complex solution when an elementary one would suffice. She felt that Carl Hayden's robot was "conceptually similar" to the machines she encountered at NASA.

The guys were in shock. They marched back up to the stage and looked out at the audience with dazed smiles. Lorenzo felt a rush of emotion. The judges' Special Prize wasn't a consolation award. These people were giving them real recognition. He thanked Merrill and headed back to his seat with the others. Now they'd really have something to talk about in Phoenix.

Before they could get off the stage, Merrill announced that they had won another prize: the Technical Writing Award.

Lorenzo didn't know what was happening. It seemed impossible that they would win three awards, particularly one for writing. *Us illiterate people from the desert?* Lorenzo thought. He looked at Cristian, who had been responsible for a large part of the writing. Even Cristian was amazed. To his analytical mind, there was no possibility that his team—a bunch of ESL students— could have produced a better written report than kids from one of the country's top engineering schools.

Merrill congratulated them. They had just won two of the most important awards. It was astonishing, but now the room was ready for the announcement of the top three overall finishers. The Carl Hayden kids returned to their seats. They were now a highly decorated underwater-robotics team. It had been an amazing run, something they'd never forget.

Merrill began the countdown. "Third place goes to Cape Fear

Community College," he said. There was a round of applause. Sea Devil 3, their ROV, was a work of art with robust capabilities and had amassed the second-highest number of mission points. The Carl Hayden kids were surprised. They had assumed that Cape Fear would grab second place. It was a given that MIT would win the championship, so they figured that Monterey Peninsula College had slid into second place. They were a solid team that had performed well underwater and likely aced the engineering review. Carl Hayden figured they might have gotten as high as fourth place. That was pretty exciting.

After the applause for Cape Fear died down, Merrill cleared his throat for the next announcement. "And second place goes to MIT," he said into the microphone.

There was a feeling of shock in the room. Cristian looked at Fredi.

"MIT got second?" Cristian blurted.

"So who won first place?" Lorenzo asked the table.

Fredi realized that something extraordinary was about to occur. He leaned across the table and grabbed Lorenzo's shirt. "Lorenzo, if what I think is about to happen does happen, I do not, under any circumstances, want to hear you say the word *Hooters* onstage."

"And the winner of the Marine Advanced Technology Education ROV Explorer-class championship goes to . . ."

Merrill started drumming on the podium. A deep rumble rose up around the room as others joined in. Only nine months earlier, the Carl Hayden students hadn't known what an ROV was. There was no way they could win.

Merrill stopped drumming.

The room fell silent, and Merrill leaned into the microphone.

"Carl Hayden!" he shouted.

The 2004 Marine Advanced Technology and Education Explorer class ROV championship was not going to a big-league university, or a team of seasoned competitors. It was going to four high school students who had simply hoped not to finish last.

"Oh my God," Allan said. He felt tears welling up. He grabbed Fredi and shook him. "Oh my God!"

Lorenzo threw his arms into the air, looked at Fredi, and silently mouthed, *Hooters*.

The students from MIT stood up and began to clap. Other competitors stood as well, and by the time the Carl Hayden team made it to the stage, most of the room was on its feet. The teenagers from Phoenix were getting a standing ovation. The audience roared their support.

The kids from the desert had won.

"WE BEAT MIT!" Cristian screamed out to the ocean. They had hiked a mile down the darkened beach. They couldn't contain themselves inside the awards hall and had gotten out as quickly as they could. They didn't want to be rude, but it was too much to handle without a little yelling.

"We wo-o-o-o-o-on!" Oscar hollered into the night sky.

"*AHHHRGH!*" Luis roared.

He was so loud, everyone fell silent. The night was quiet—just the sound of the waves crashing softly.

"I want you guys to know how proud I am of you," Allan said.

"From now on, you guys are the team that beat MIT," Fredi told them. "You know what that makes you?"

"What?" Cristian asked.

"Badasses," Fredi said, smiling.

"Damn," Lorenzo said, getting used to the idea. "I'm a badass."

Oscar couldn't remember being happier, but his eighteenth birthday was only days away. It brought a significant decision for him. Once he turned eighteen and became an adult in the eyes of the law, his legal status in the United States would change. He was always at risk of deportation, but as a youth, he couldn't be banned from reentering the country. However, if he was caught and deported after he turned eighteen and a half, he would be barred from returning to the United States for three years. If he was nineteen and a half or older and caught, the ban would increase to ten years. The law was meant to incentivize immigrant teens to return to the country where they were born.

But, for Oscar, there was little to go back to. He remembered

Mexico—he'd left when he was twelve—but there was nothing there for him anymore. His parents were in Arizona, as were his friends and mentors. It was hard to imagine walking across the border to Mexico in a week's time when his entire life was in the United States. And fundamentally, he viewed himself as an American. He figured that he would eventually be able to convince the government that he was worthy of citizenship.

Fredi took a picture of the kids standing by the shore that night. Oscar, Cristian, and Lorenzo threw their fists in the air. Oscar held up his index finger to signal that they were number one. Luis looked confused. On the beach around them, piles of shrimp had been washed ashore. There were hundreds that had been overpowered by forces beyond their control. Fredi took pictures of everything that night so nobody would ever forget.

FOUR

ON DECEMBER 16, 2004—five months after the Carl Hayden triumph in Santa Barbara—Russell Pearce took the stage at the Brookings Institution's Falk Auditorium in Washington, D.C. The Arizona state representative had been invited to talk about policies affecting children in immigrant families. The session was titled "The Future of Children," and Pearce expressed his strong belief that being too nice to immigrants wasn't good for the country or even the immigrants themselves.

"You don't have a right to have compassion," Pearce insisted. "None of us would do anything to harm children. But sometimes our policies, well intended, do much damage."

To Pearce, Arizona and the United States had become too hospitable to immigrants. They were flooding the country, illegally receiving welfare, and getting a free education at taxpayers' expense. Many voters in Arizona seemed to believe that immigrants had come to the country to leech off the government. From this perspective, immigrants weren't here looking for work, they were poor, lazy families that would contribute less than they received to the country. Pearce felt that policies needed to be put in place to discourage them from entering the United States.

Pearce championed a solution. Just a month before his speech in D.C., voters in Arizona had passed Proposition 200, a bill that barred illegal immigrants from receiving public benefits, from welfare to education. The text of the proposition summarized the motivation succinctly: "This state finds that illegal immigration is causing economic hardship to this state and that illegal immigration is encouraged by public agencies within this state that provide public benefits without verifying immigration status." Fifty-six percent of voters voted in favor of the proposition and it passed.

Sheriff Joe Arpaio responded to the rising tide of anti-immigrant sentiment among voters in Phoenix by forming civilian posses to hunt for illegal immigrants. Starting in 2006, the posses were made up of more than three hundred civilians who were encouraged to track down illegal migrants. They were told to identify cars that appeared to be carrying illegal immigrants, as well as houses where they lived. Though they were only supposed to turn the information over to sheriff's deputies, many of the volunteers were armed. Both opponents and supporters of the posses saw them as a way of scaring migrants out of the country.

Far from cooling down, the debate over immigration was only getting more heated. On May 15, 2006, President Bush ordered six thousand members of the National Guard to begin patrols of the U.S.-Mexican border. The intent was to buttress the Border Patrol's efforts to capture immigrants and prevent migrants from crossing. "The reason why I think this strategy is important is because deploying the six thousand troops to complement the work of the Border Patrol will get immediate results," Bush said. "And it's time to get immediate results."

The question was: Would militarizing the border achieve the desired results? "It's as if we expect border control agents to do what a century of communism could not: defeat the natural market forces of supply and demand and defeat the natural human desire for freedom and opportunity," noted New York mayor Michael Bloomberg told Congress. "You might as well sit in your beach chair and tell the tide not to come in."

OSCAR WIPED the white gypsum dust from his face. It was a hot Tuesday afternoon in Phoenix eight months after the success in Santa Barbara. The half-built apartment complex in front of him was teeming with workers. He was wearing a leather carpenter's belt slung with a hammer, and he lifted a four-foot-by-twelve-foot section of Sheetrock from a pile. He may have proven himself to be one of the most innovative underwater engineers in the country, but now he was just another day laborer.

He had chosen to stay in the United States past his eighteenth birthday and now felt stuck: there was nothing for him in Mexico, and he was like a ghost in the United States. He was running the risk of being banned from the country for years. Still, Oscar maintained a sense of optimism. As he trudged through the half-built units hauling hundred-pound sections of drywall, he studied the plumbing and electrical wiring. He wanted to make sure he was learning something.

In the heat, when he let his thoughts wander, he thought about college. He dreamed that he would major in mechanical engineering, serve in the military, and go on to have a career as an engineer. It all seemed like a mirage, since he couldn't afford the first step. He was making between five and eight dollars an hour, and a degree from Arizona State University would cost approximately fifty thousand dollars. There was no way he could raise that kind of money by sheetrocking.

Cristian had a similar problem. He also dreamed of going to college, but his hopes flagged when the air-conditioning unit in his family's trailer broke. Without AC, the trailer turned into an unlivable aluminum oven in the desert heat. His parents had to spend three thousand dollars of savings to buy a new unit—money that Cristian had hoped could be used to at least start college.

After graduation, Luis started working two jobs. During the day, he filed papers at a Social Security office. In the evenings, he continued to work as a short-order cook for Harold Brunet at Doc's Dining & Bar in Youngtown. It seemed unrealistic to expect that his life would change that much. He assumed that Santa Barbara had been nothing more than a blip, a brief glimpse into the opportunities that other people had. He tried not to think too much about it.

In April 2005, I published an article in *Wired* detailing the 2004 MATE championship in Santa Barbara. It was the first national coverage of the event, and the story provoked a variety of responses. Hooters called to invite the entire robotics team to a free dinner. ("That was hella cool," Lorenzo recalls.) Many readers wrote to express their support for the Carl Hayden robotics program.

"If the really long list of immigrant inventors who have made this country and the world a much better place is to stop here and now, we will also likely become the newest declining nation," one reader commented.

The *Wired* office was soon flooded by e-mails offering to help the four young roboticists continue their education. Individual readers eventually contributed more than $120,000 to a scholarship fund set up by the school district for these kids. This generosity opened up a world of opportunity for them. It now looked like college was within their grasp.

The article also made the four Carl Hayden teens the faces of a generation of kids who were born elsewhere and had grown up without residency papers in the United States. In 2004, there were an estimated 1.4 million kids who fit this description. Despite their numbers, these children were largely invisible. Their families avoided publicity. After all, nobody wanted to invite scrutiny if it meant deportation.

At first, the Carl Hayden team didn't realize that their story would attract much notice. Nobody had paid attention when they first won the MATE competition, so they figured the *Wired* article wouldn't change anything. But in the weeks following publication, additional media requests poured in. When ABC's *Nightline* asked to broadcast their story, the teammates had a meeting in the robotics closet. Fredi and Allan explained that the show wanted to focus on their immigration status. They were being asked to talk about living illegally in the country on national television. It could lead to trouble for all of them.

"If you were my own kids, I would tell you not to do it," Allan said. "It's too risky."

After discussing with their families overnight, the teens reconvened the next day. They agreed that if any one of them didn't want to do it, they would say no to ABC. Cristian's family was very concerned and didn't want him to participate. He wasn't convinced though. Cristian thought that it was important to speak out. Lorenzo and Luis agreed. They needed to talk about their experience. Otherwise, traditional stereotypes about immigrants would persist. Voters naturally fell back on their assumptions about what low-income Mexican migrants were like. Stories of migrants stealing or fighting made the news, but when Carl Hayden won the national underwater-robotics championship, no prominent news outlet covered the story initially.

"We got a chance to say something," Lorenzo said.

"I agree," Oscar said. "This is a Rosa Parks moment. It's about more than us now."

They decided to do the broadcast.

THE MEDIA ATTENTION prompted some to wonder if Santa Barbara had just been a fluke, a one-time accident of fate. Cristian and Lorenzo—who hadn't yet graduated—proved them wrong. In 2005 and 2006, the Carl Hayden robotics team won the top prize at Dean Kamen's Arizona FIRST competition in Arizona. They went on to the national championships both years and were a top competitor. They placed third at the 2005 MATE event and second at the 2006 event, beating MIT (again) both times. In 2007, MATE organizers held the event in Canada, in effect preventing the undocumented students at Carl Hayden from attending. To compensate, Fredi and Allan formed their own underwater-robotics competition, an event that continues to this day.

More than anything, the 2004 underwater-robotics team inspired the kids that came after them. The robotics team swelled to more than fifty members, all of whom heard the tale of how Oscar, Luis, Lorenzo, and Cristian had succeeded with little more than their ingenuity and some spare parts. Now, when the team competed, the cheerleaders showed up. In 2008, the team won the national Chairman's Award, the most prestigious prize at Kamen's FIRST competition. Year after year, they consistently performed at or near the top of every division they entered.

They also tried to get other kids excited about robotics. During the fall, before the year's serious robot building got underway, team members fanned out to local elementary schools in West Phoenix. They brought old robots with them and gave demonstrations to the younger kids. In 2004, the Carl Hayden robotics team hosted a junior robotics competition in their gym. Within a few years, the event grew to include hundreds of young students and had to be relocated to Arizona State University.

The team's rising profile brought new supporters. In 2005, a group of businessmen in Oregon and Washington read the *Wired* article and decided to help. They formed a foundation that provided college scholarships for members of Allan and Fredi's robotics team. Between 2005 and 2010, the foundation spent $720,000 and sent twenty-three kids to college. "Our country cannot afford to squander the talents of these kids," says Peter Gaskins, one of the businessmen. "I'm just not willing to accept that this is the way it has to be."

The robotics program became a pathway to college. Robotics students won more scholarships than all of Carl Hayden's athletic programs combined. "This team has transformed so deeply that expectations, dreams, and possibilities have expanded beyond what was previously unimaginable," said John Abele, the billionaire cofounder of Boston Scientific, in announcing the top award at Dean Kamen's 2008 robotics competition. "What was once a struggling school is now a soaring inspiration that demonstrates a passionate partnership . . . can unlock the dreams hidden within."

Fredi and Allan may have succeeded in giving their immigrant students new dreams, but often the reality was that those dreams were impractical. Many Carl Hayden students didn't have Social Security numbers or green cards and couldn't get normal jobs even if they did graduate from college. It kept Fredi up at night. He worried that his kids would drop out of the program if they felt that it wasn't going to lead to better lives. In his mind, that led to a ripple effect of catastrophic proportions. Kids would drop out of school entirely if they didn't see the point, crime would increase, society would lose great minds, and the next generation wouldn't be prepared to take over the country. At least that's what went through his mind late at night. He might be able to inspire and train extraordinary engineers, but the world didn't seem to want them.

ALLAN AND FREDI urged Cristian to apply to MIT; it seemed like a natural fit. But to Cristian and his family, Boston seemed too far away, too foreign. His parents wanted to keep him close given his residency status. They felt better having him nearby. A private university also seemed forbiddingly expensive.

Arizona State University was a safer choice. Cristian would qualify for in-state tuition and would be able to cover the costs with the scholarship windfall. Still, ASU was a difficult departure from Carl Hayden. Cristian found himself in lectures with almost four hundred students. His chemistry teacher stood in front of the lecture hall and read the slides he projected onto a screen. It was mind-numbing and infuriating, particularly because 10 percent of the chemistry grade was tied to attendance. It felt like the antithesis to four years of building robots at Carl Hayden.

Since his parents hadn't gone to college, he found it hard to share his feelings with them. Instead, he regularly stopped by Carl Hayden to talk to Allan and Fredi. "I'm not learning anything, but I have to show up anyway," he fumed on one occasion. "It's a huge waste of time."

"You have to jump through the hoops," Allan told him. "It'll be worth it."

Cristian stuck with it, but statewide sentiment was turning against him. When ABC's *Nightline* aired their segment on the Carl Hayden kids, Arizona State Representative Russell Pearce explained to viewers that it was inappropriate to focus on a small group of students: "You can't paint this picture of this sweet child over here that we all probably know. And all of us know somebody that's here probably illegally that is a wonderful, wonderful person. You can't take it to that emotional element and, and let that play. Because, look at the damage to America overall."

Midway through Cristian's freshman year, Dean Martin, an Arizona state senator, sponsored Proposition 300, an effort to extend Proposition 200's ban on public services for undocumented immigrants to education. The referendum sought to prevent state colleges and universities from offering reduced in-state tuition to undocumented residents who'd grown up in Arizona. "Arizona is currently giving away millions of your tax dollars as subsidies to illegals," Martin wrote in a ballot argument sent to voters. "U.S. citizens from other states attending Arizona schools have to pay the full cost of tuition. However, citizens of foreign countries, who break the law to enter Arizona illegally, are given taxpayer subsidized tuition . . . It's not fair; it's not right."

Russell Pearce was an outspoken proponent of the new measure. "Free state services for all takes away the incentive for illegal aliens to become full citizens and legitimate members of American society," Pearce wrote in support of Proposition 300. "It is vital that we spend our tax dollars on helping Arizonans and not aid and abet illegal aliens."

On November 7, 2006, Proposition 300 passed with 71 percent support. Cristian's tuition quadrupled as a result. Normally, one year of residency in Arizona would qualify a student for in-state tuition. Cristian had lived in the state since the age of five but was now deemed to be an out-of-state student. His first-semester tuition was about $2,000, but the next semester was now going to cost roughly $8,000. To get through the remaining three and a half years of college, he would need $56,000. His share of the scholarship money would get him only halfway through to a degree. If he took only two classes, he wouldn't trigger the tuition increase, but the mechanical-engineering department required students to take a full load of classes to remain in the program. It seemed hopeless. He decided to drop out.

Technically, he should have returned to Mexico. Once there, he could apply for a visa, though if he admitted that he had stayed in the United States beyond his eighteenth birthday, he would be banned from reentering the country for years. He hadn't been in Mexico since he was a young child: it was a foreign country to him. He couldn't bring himself to leave the United States.

For the next five years, Cristian took intermittent courses at Gateway Community College. He found work at Home Depot and was assigned to the floor-and-wall department, where he helped customers order carpets and blinds. When someone bought a particularly large order of tile, he would walk in front of the forklift waving a flag to clear a path down the aisles.

At home, he set up a small laboratory in the corner of his room. He bought a soldering iron for thirty dollars and kept his eye out for deals at Home Depot. When two hundred feet of doorbell wire went on sale for three dollars, he bought himself a spool and brought it home. Most nights, he stayed up late, inventing new machines from scavenged parts. He found a broken guitar on the street, repaired it, and made a sound-effects pedal for it. He designed a new wheel that could rotate in any direction. He kept a gallon of muriatic acid beside his bed to etch circuit boards. At night, amid the smell of solder and machine oil, he felt most happy.

IN MAY 2006, Lorenzo walked up to the stage in the auditorium at Carl Hayden to receive his diploma. He was the first member of his family to graduate from high school. It should have been a happy day. At one time, Principal Ybarra was on the verge of expelling him. Now he was a nationally recognized robotics star. But as Lorenzo shook hands with Ybarra onstage and accepted the diploma, he scanned the crowd. His father hadn't shown up.

Lorenzo tamped down his feelings and tried to focus on his future. With his share of the scholarship money, he enrolled full-time in Phoenix College's Culinary Studies program and went on to receive an associate's degree after two years. Luis also went to cooking school, attending the Cordon Bleu College of Culinary Arts in nearby Scottsdale. Together, the two friends formed Neither Here, Nor There, a catering company that specialized in Mexican-fusion dining. They started with their mothers' recipes but revamped them, turning a traditional green mole sauce into a mole pesto by adding basil, pine nuts, and cream. They catered weddings, church retreats, baby showers, and quinceañeras. It was fun but intermittent, and both had to get steadier jobs. Luis found work as a night-shift janitor at the federal courthouse in downtown Phoenix. From nine at night until five in the morning, he wandered the halls of justice with a trash cart and buffed the marble floors. Lorenzo got a job as a dishwasher at St. Francis, an upscale restaurant in central Phoenix.

Lorenzo's added income wasn't enough to save his family's home and, in 2009, Lorenzo handed the keys over to the Realtor who had bought the property. The guy walked through the house and was astounded by the state of poverty the family had been living in. The building was poorly built to begin with, but now the walls were discolored from years of use. The Realtor got the distinct impression that bugs were crawling on him and hurriedly left. On his way home, he bought a bottle of rubbing alcohol and doused his legs and feet. He couldn't imagine how anyone would live there. But to Lorenzo, it was his home.

While the kids from Carl Hayden struggled to get by, the second-place winners of the 2004 MATE competition excelled. Thaddeus Stefanov-Wagner, the student who had rebuilt MIT's electronics in a week, landed a job as a mechanical engineer at Bluefin Robotics. The company was founded by MIT alumni and built self-piloting ROVs for commercial, military, and scientific customers. Jordan Stanway, the team leader in 2004, got a Ph.D. in oceanography from MIT and the Woods Hole Oceanographic Institution and builds underwater robots for the Monterey Bay Aquarium Research Institute. Other team members went on to work at NASA and ExxonMobil. They were all exceptionally talented students and deserved to do well.

Meanwhile, in Phoenix, Lorenzo's dishwashing abilities impressed his superiors, who promoted him to prep cook and then line cook. On a typical Friday night at the restaurant, the airy dining room fills with well-dressed patrons. There are exposed roof beams, rough-hewn brick and concrete walls, and a roll-up, see-through garage door. Like many hip restaurants, it feels as if someone spent a lot of time and money to make it look rustic and down-trodden.

The patrons tend to ignore the cooks, who are clearly visible in the open kitchen. Lorenzo stands there for hours every day roasting salmon and pork chops. He's also responsible for the prosciutto-fig-and-goat flatbread and the Moroccan meatballs. He sends out dozens of plates every day for customers who appreciate the pleasant tang in the chile verde sauce and the crunch of the stuffed peppers. They eat the food never knowing the history of the twenty-five-year-old robotics expert who cooked it.

IN FEBRUARY 2005—before the response to the *Wired* article provided him with enough money to start college—Oscar stopped by a friend's house in West Phoenix and met the guy's cousin. Karla Perez was visiting from El Mirage, a town northwest of Phoenix, where she was a junior at Dysart High School. Oscar couldn't stop watching her. She was only sixteen, but her pencil-thin eyebrows made her look older, and she had a half smile that seemed to say, *I know what you're up to and I'm not buying it.* Oscar was smitten.

For her part, Karla fell for Oscar immediately. She appreciated the way he dressed—button-up shirts with no wrinkles, polished leather shoes. He looked serious and respectable even though he was only eighteen. She watched as Oscar and his cousin raced remote-control cars down the street. Oscar seemed so sure of himself, so confident, even when horsing around. "This is a man who is going places," she thought.

That night, they piled into the friend's yellow Mustang convertible to meet up with some friends. Oscar ended up in the back with Karla. Somebody handed him a camcorder and told him to record the evening. Oscar leaned out the back and started taping. When they hit a bump, Karla instinctively reached up and grabbed his butt, pulling him back in by the pocket. It was awkward and funny. They both laughed.

Over the next few months, both continued to make excuses to visit Karla's cousin's house, where they knew they'd see each other. Karla's family approved of Oscar and encouraged the relationship. "That's the type of guy we like," Karla's aunt told her.

Somehow, when it was time to drive Karla back across town, everybody else in the family would suddenly be busy. Oscar would find himself driving her twenty miles back to El Mirage. It was nice, at least until his car broke down. He didn't have the money to fix it, which slowed the nascent romance.

In April 2005, Karla tried to get things back on track by asking Oscar if he would like to take her to prom. She was sure he would say yes. In her mind, it was going to be the night they kissed and started dating. They would get married, have kids, and always look back on the night as the start of their relationship. Unfortunately, Oscar said he couldn't go.

"What?" Karla demanded. She was hurt, suspicious, and angry.

"I can't afford to take you," Oscar said. "And if I can't pay for it, I can't go."

Karla was disappointed but also loved him more for it. Oscar's integrity was one of the things that drew her to him. Though she was a U.S. citizen, she knew Oscar was in the country illegally. She also knew that he struggled with the predicament that he found himself in. His parents had brought him here when he was a child, and he had grown up as an Arizonan. Legally, he was now supposed to leave America for a country he barely knew. He could then apply for a green card once he was back in Mexico, but in his budding relationship with Karla he had found yet another reason to stay.

Karla decided to go to her prom anyway—it was her big night after all—but she skipped out after a couple of hours and found Oscar at a small Mexican restaurant called El Pitic, near the airport. She was wearing her prom dress—a luxurious, white, frilly thing. She looked radiant amid the discolored ceiling tiles of the strip-mall restaurant. They left together and, later that night, at a friend's house, kissed for the first time. Seven months later, they were married.

THE MONEY SENT in by *Wired* readers allowed Oscar to enroll full-time at Arizona State University starting in the fall of 2005. He decided to major in mechanical engineering and poured himself into his course work. It was intellectually challenging, but he felt detached from the real world. Fundamentally, he missed building things. He assumed that the university would have a robotics team, but to his surprise there wasn't one.

Carl Hayden had trained Oscar well. To start a team, he needed an adviser, so he quickly scheduled a meeting with Antonio Garcia, a professor in ASU's school of engineering. Oscar explained how formative his robotics experiences had been. Competitions were a great way to help students apply their classroom learning. Plus, it was just fun.

"How can I help?" Garcia said.

"I'd like a grant to form a team."

It was easy to say yes to someone like Oscar. By the end of the meeting, the ASU RoboDevils were born with the support of the engineering department. The team's success would spawn other robotics teams at the university, including an all-women's robotics squad. But, at the outset in 2005, it was just Oscar and a handful of other mechanical-engineering students.

By his sophomore year, Oscar had established himself as a standout student leader. He was the captain of the RoboDevils and traveled to high schools around Phoenix to talk to kids about forming their own robotics teams. He had been featured on ABC's *Nightline* program, discussing his robotics accomplishments and immigration challenges. Karla was also pregnant with their first child. Everything seemed to be going right in his life.

But nothing could change the fact that he was still an immigrant with no visa or permanent residency. Even though he was married to a U.S. citizen and would soon have a daughter who would also be a U.S. citizen, the fact that he had stayed in the country past his eighteenth birthday marked him. This doomed any residency or citizenship claim he could make.

The political atmosphere also complicated his life as Proposition 300 threatened to end his college career early. The referendum had succeeded in driving Cristian out of school, but Cristian was just one of thousands of new freshman. He didn't stand out yet. Oscar had already distinguished himself at the university, and a consortium of groups rallied to fund his education. The Ira A. Fulton Schools of Engineering at Arizona State University and Chicanos por la Causa chipped in money, as did Luis, who allocated a portion of his scholarship money to Oscar's education. Luis was attending the Cordon Bleu College of Culinary Arts and wasn't going to need all the money, so he gave his remaining share to Oscar. By the end of his sophomore year, Oscar had commitments to fund his remaining two years at ASU.

On May 13, 2009, President Obama stepped onto the stage at Sun Devil Stadium to give the graduation speech for ASU's fiftieth commencement. The stadium was jammed with more than seventy thousand people. It was the largest graduation ceremony in American history. The president's arrival was such a draw, students were reportedly scalping their tickets on Craigslist for thirty-packs of Bud Light.

To Oscar, the idea of missing his own, hard-earned graduation for some beer was laughable. Though it was hot—the temperature reached 110 in the late afternoon and a dozen people were rushed to the hospital—Oscar looked sharp and fresh in a crisp blue button-up shirt, a classic black gown, and a cap with a yellow tassel. He was ready to graduate.

Part of his excitement was due to a secret. He hadn't told Karla or his parents that he was one of three seniors out of a class of more than nine thousand to receive "special honors" as an outstanding member of the class of 2009. The graduation organizers had reserved a spot for Oscar near Obama. When the commencement began, Christine Wilkinson, the university's senior vice president, took the podium and, to Karla's amazement, called on Oscar to stand up in front of President Obama and the entire seventy-thousand-person crowd.

Oscar stood with a giant, embarrassed smile.

"Oh my God," Karla shrieked from the grandstands. "That's my husband!"

"In the spring of 2004, Oscar and his three teammates took it all," Wilkinson said. She described Oscar's success in Santa Barbara, noting that his team triumphed due to their "ingenuity, positive outlook, and willingness to work hard."

"That's my husband!" Karla shrieked again.

"He is known as a leader, the motivator of his team." Wilkinson cited his desire to enlist but noted that an "immigration technicality" had derailed both his education and military career. Robotics, she said, helped his flagging spirits during that time and had kept him focused on his education despite the challenges. Now he had crossed the finish line.

"He will graduate with a bachelor of science degree in mechanical engineering," Wilkinson said as the crowd cheered and the president clapped approvingly. "Congratulations, Oscar."

After an introduction from ASU's president, Obama took the podium and told the seniors that they were entering a world of "upheaval." Two wars were ongoing and the financial crisis was causing turmoil around the world. But he wanted his audience to know that there was hope.

"I know starting your careers in troubled times is a challenge," Obama said. "But it is also a privilege. Because it's moments like these that force us to try harder, to dig deeper, and to discover gifts we never knew we had—to find the greatness that lies within each of us. So don't ever shy away from that endeavor. Don't stop adding to your body of work. I can promise that you will be the better for that continued effort, as will this nation that we all love."

Oscar listened intently. He was now twenty-two years old and had spent a decade in the United States. He had an American wife and an American daughter, and had built a life in Phoenix. But that made him more vulnerable than ever, as he risked losing everything he loved by being deported. He might be graduating with a valuable degree in mechanical engineering, and the president of the United States might have applauded his accomplishments, but Oscar was still a hunted man.

He decided to do what Obama had asked of the class of 2009, to not shy away from finding his own greatness. He decided to deport himself.

ON SEPTEMBER 1, 2009, Oscar walked back into Mexico for the first time in ten years. The Greyhound that brought him to El Paso faded away behind him as he walked across the bridge leading to Juárez, Mexico. Below, the Rio Grande was a sickly black trickle. The Mexicans knew better than to call it grand. For years, farmers on both sides of the border had siphoned off much of the water. That it still existed at all was a surprise. In Mexico, it was called the Río Bravo—the Brave River.

Karla came with Oscar and left the baby with her mother. She wanted to support him, though she was nervous. In 2009, Juárez was ranked the most dangerous city in the world, often posting more than a hundred murders every week. To Karla, it was like stepping back into a lawless, impoverished time. The cars in Juárez were twenty years older, the roads were ragged, and many windows were covered with plywood. Motorists ignored the streetlights and swerved wildly across all lanes. It seemed dangerous just to walk on the sidewalk. Karla clung to Oscar's arm.

Oscar remained stoic. He didn't want to let his emotions take over. On the far side of the bridge, they got into a taxi and drove to a medical clinic a block from the U.S. consulate. Applicants for residency had to have a clean bill of health, so Oscar gave blood and had an X-ray taken of his chest. He was found to be in perfect shape. At least from that perspective, he was an ideal candidate for citizenship.

They checked into the Quality Inn, a hotel on the same block as the consulate. The lady at the front desk warned them not to stray far: "This block around the consulate is okay. But don't go farther than that." She also told them to get to the consulate early—the line could stretch around the block.

They woke at dawn. Oscar felt terrible; he was coming down with the flu, but he tried to ignore it. They walked down the street in the dark. Hundreds of people were already lined up. Oscar and Karla took a spot in the queue and waited. When the sun came up, it got hot. The line inched forward a little every hour. After five hours, it was Oscar's turn. Applicants weren't allowed inside the walls of the consulate. They just arrived at a small, bulletproof window cut into the wall. Oscar leaned in. A man was sitting on the other side.

"I'd like to apply for residency," Oscar said.

"Documents?" the clerk said, sounding tired.

Oscar slid his application and medical certification through a slot. The man flipped through the packet and saw that Oscar was married to an American and had an American daughter. He asked Oscar to confirm the date of his marriage and the spelling of his daughter's name.

Then the clerk posed a simple question: "Were you ever illegally in the United States?"

Oscar could have simply said no. The consulate checks for a criminal record but doesn't have the time to dig up the minutiae of every applicant's life. It was possible that they would turn up a record of his ASU graduation, or some other telltale sign that he had been living in the United States, but admitting that he had been in the United States would guarantee the rejection of his application.

But Oscar refused to lie. He didn't want his path to citizenship to be based on fraud. He wanted America to want him. He hoped for understanding so he looked at the man and told the truth: "Yes. My parents brought me to the United States illegally when I was twelve, and I lived there until crossing back yesterday."

"Your application will be denied," the man said mechanically.

It felt like a slap across the face. But then the clerk explained that Oscar could apply for a waiver. It was his only hope. He would have to demonstrate that being separated from his family would cause extreme hardship for his wife and child. Since they were both U.S. citizens, the government might seek to mitigate their pain. The clerk told Oscar he could come back in eleven weeks and present his case. In the meantime, he was stuck in Mexico.

OSCAR STEPPED OFF the bus in Temosachic. In his memory, his former hometown was a pristine rural community. Now it appeared to be an abandoned cluster of crumbled homes by the side of a state highway. It looked dirty and depopulated. He walked down the main street and saw boarded-up houses. Many of his neighbors had long since departed for the United States, giving the place the feel of a ghost town.

Oscar found his childhood home. The grass had grown up tall all around it, and through the dirt-caked windows, he could see that the inside was covered in spiderwebs. He shook the metal door. It was locked. He didn't have a key so he wandered down to a tire shop on the main road run by an old friend of the family's. Together, they walked back, knocked the door off its hinges, installed a new lock, and put the door back on the front of the house.

Oscar moved in and set about making the most of his time. He cleaned up the family home and got a job picking beans for about $3.80 a day. It wasn't what he expected to be doing after graduating with a degree in mechanical engineering. In the mornings, the temperature hovered around freezing and it was hard to get his fingers around the stalks of the plants. As the sun rose, the temperature rose dramatically, sometimes passing ninety. After about six hours of picking, he was soaked in sweat, but he worked fast. He still wanted to be the best, even if that meant he was the best bean picker.

Eleven weeks later, Karla stood nervously at the bus station in

Juárez. She hadn't seen Oscar for almost three months and scanned the crowd for her husband. She saw a stocky man walking toward her and tensed. He was wearing boots made out of discarded car tires and jeans splattered with mud. He kept his face down, his eyes hidden beneath a soiled, faded-gold Arizona State University baseball cap.

"Oscar?" Karla said tentatively.

Oscar looked up, smiled, and wrapped her in his arms. He had put on muscle working in the fields and was trim underneath his shirt. Karla felt butterflies, as if she were a teenager falling in love all over again. "What are you doing looking like that?" she chided. "You stink."

They headed for a taxi and Oscar explained that he was trying to blend in. He didn't want to look American and attract the attention of thieves or gangsters. The stink came from the pound of cheese in his backpack. He'd made it himself and hoped that the pungent aroma would convince people that he was nothing more than an impoverished peasant.

Karla had come prepared. They checked into the Quality Inn and she unpacked Oscar's wedding suit. He showered and came out looking great. Clean-cut, strong, and handsome. It was the first time he'd worn the suit since their wedding. "Oh, wow," Karla thought. "Look at this guy." She was sure that America would want him.

She also prayed that the government would understand. Karla was working constantly at an Alamo Rent A Car office at the airport in Phoenix. Her salary was all the money they had. At four dollars a day, Oscar's bean picking did little to help. As it was, Karla couldn't afford to buy enough food and send Oscar money for bus tickets. She had begun accepting charity from a Phoenix-area food bank to feed herself and her one-year-old. The time she was taking off now to be with Oscar only worsened their predicament. She desperately wanted Oscar back.

After six hours in line, Oscar presented himself at the consulate's bulletproof window again. He tried to straighten his suit; it had lost some of its crispness over the hours standing in the sun. Oscar didn't let that dampen his spirits though. He stood tall, his tie knotted perfectly in a half Windsor, and slid the clerk his I-601 form. It was termed an "Application for Waiver of Grounds of Inadmissibility." Oscar included a copy of his ASU diploma, a reprint from the Arizona House of Representatives' official record honoring his accomplishments, and letters of support from Karla, Allan, and Fredi. The clerk was nonplussed.

"When I had to leave Oscar in Juárez, it was like leaving a piece of me behind," Karla wrote the government. "We have been good people who work extremely hard for the few things that we have . . . We do not deserve to have our family torn apart. Please I beg of you to grant Oscar Vazquez the right to live and work in the USA with his family. He just wants to provide for us and have a loving home for our children to grow up in."

The clerk took the paperwork and told Oscar that the government would issue a decision in seven to ten days.

"Thank you, sir," Oscar said.

A WEEK LATER, Oscar received word that the decision was waiting for him at a local DHL office. He and Karla hurriedly got in a taxi for the twelve-minute ride. The cabbie often drove this route, doing a brisk business ferrying would-be immigrants from the consulate to the courier company. Oftentimes, he would wait to bring clients back to their hotel, so he had witnessed many people's dreams come true. The return in those cases felt like a celebration. He had also driven clients back in complete silence, a heavy pall hanging over the cab.

"I can tell you this," the driver said to Oscar on the way to the office. "If the packet is thick, it's good news. If it's thin, it's not."

The driver dropped them inside the gated DHL facility and parked in the large parking lot, which had room enough to accommodate all the taxis that idled while people learned their fates. Karla took Oscar's hand and they walked inside, showed Oscar's ID, and received a thin envelope. Karla felt the tears welling up. Oscar opened the envelope in a daze.

"You have been found ineligible for a visa," the letter inside read.

Oscar had received the maximum penalty: he was banned from the United States for a decade.

KARLA RETURNED TO PHOENIX on the Greyhound, sobbing most of the way. She barely remembers saying goodbye to Oscar in Juárez. He just disappeared.

Oscar knew there was nothing for him in Temosachic, and Juárez was too dangerous. With few good ideas, he boarded a bus for Magdalena, a town an hour south of the Arizona border. An uncle of Karla's lived there; it was better than nothing. Oscar rented a one-room concrete structure by a dried-up riverbed and walked to local businesses to apply for a job. He wasn't the only one looking for work. After two weeks, he hadn't found anything, but he heard that a car-parts factory just outside town was hiring.

He lined up with a dozen other applicants at the factory gate and got an appointment for an interview the following day. He showed up with his résumé and ASU diploma.

The interviewer seemed surprised. "You're pretty well educated."

"Yes, sir, but I'm willing to take any job."

"We only have low-level assembly-line positions. You're over-qualified for that."

"I'm happy to do anything." Oscar's aspirations were in tatters. He no longer dreamed of doing important work or building cutting-edge robots. He had no contacts or money and had to build a life in a country he didn't know. That was challenge enough.

He was hired to supervise a portion of the assembly line and began building wire harnesses, the bundles of cables that run behind dashboards and underneath a car's seats. He was paid about $22 a day. It was better than picking beans, but it was far from ideal. After a month, he managed to get an Internet connection and started looking for opportunities in other countries. He knew Germans appreciated good engineering talent, and he wasn't barred from moving there. Maybe he could move the family to Europe if America didn't want him.

At night, he called Karla and tried to sound chipper. It was hard. Intermittent gun battles occurred in the streets, and Oscar had to crouch low by the walls inside his hovel. The bullets pinged off his metal roof and thudded into the concrete walls. He flipped off the lights and hoped nobody would try to break in. One morning, he walked outside and saw eight bodies in the streets. Oscar told Karla that he was having trouble staying optimistic. "I'm so lonely," he said.

On one of his first days off, he spoke to Allan on the phone. "This is just totally unbelievable," Allan said. "I'm so sorry."

"I'm doing fine." Oscar didn't want Allan to worry about him.

"That's good to hear," Allan said cheerfully. He didn't want the conversation to depress his former star student.

Debbie snatched the phone away from her husband. In her opinion, Allan wasn't asking the right questions. She quizzed Oscar on his living conditions. Oscar had to admit that he was sleeping on the floor and had no furniture.

"Well, that's one thing we can change," she announced, and told Allan to get their truck ready for a journey. Debbie loaded it up with everything she could imagine Oscar would need to start a life in Mexico: a bed, sheets, towels, a TV, dishes, pans, chairs, and a couch. Karla drove to a PetSmart and bought two guinea pigs; she hoped the animals would help Oscar feel less lonely. The furry rodents rode atop a giant pile of stuff in the back of Allan's white Toyota Tundra for the four-hour drive from Phoenix to Magdalena.

Oscar found it hard to fully express how much their arrival

meant to him. It was a reminder of whom he used to be, of the kid who dreamed of doing great things. "Thank you. I just . . ."

Debbie smothered him in a hug and patted him on the back as he fought back tears.

"You're not alone," she said. "We're going to get through this together."

OSCAR'S SUPPORTERS all over the country started a letter-writing campaign to convince the government to reverse its decision. CNN picked up the story, as did *The Arizona Republic*. "Isn't he the type of person though that you would want to have immigrate to the county?" asked CNN host John Zarrella. "People who have a good education, people who have high-functioning skills like an engineering degree?"

In Washington, D.C., Oscar's story caught the attention of Senator Dick Durbin. Durbin and the Republican senator Orrin Hatch believed that America was squandering an extraordinary resource by overlooking the talents of people like Oscar. In 2001, Durbin had introduced legislation that would provide a pathway to citizenship for young immigrants who had been in the United States for at least five years and were attending college. It was titled the Development, Relief, and Education for Alien Minors Act, otherwise known as the DREAM Act. "The DREAM Act would allow a select group of immigrant students with great potential to contribute more fully to America," Durbin said.

The bill initially failed to even make it to a vote. Durbin tried every year thereafter and yet didn't make much progress. Some senators argued against it because they wanted comprehensive immigration reform, not just piecemeal legislation. Other senators had graver concerns. They believed the DREAM Act would provide amnesty and encourage migration from Mexico.

In the fall of 2010, Durbin tried again to convince senators to move forward on the bill. Almost a decade had elapsed since he first introduced the legislation and he was finally able to bring it to a vote. Durbin decided that putting a face on the plight of these kids might help. He chose to talk about Oscar and unveiled a poster-size photo of the young engineer on the floor of the U.S. Senate.

"This is Oscar Vazquez," Durbin told his colleagues. He explained that Oscar and his teammates had beaten MIT to win a robotics contest sponsored by NASA. He also said that Oscar had left the country. "This extraordinary young man—a mechanical engineer who won a national competition, a person who can add something to America, who has a wife and family here, who is doing the right thing by going back to the country of his origin even though he has little connection with it anymore—is being told: America doesn't need you," Durbin said.

The emotional plea didn't change the outcome. Senate Republicans commenced a filibuster, blocking the vote. "This bill is a law that at its fundamental core is a reward for illegal activity," said Alabama Senator Jeff Sessions, defending the filibuster. Democrats needed sixty votes to break the deadlock. They were able to muster only fifty-five votes, and the legislation was tabled yet again.

Durbin felt that it wasn't fair to students whose parents had brought them as children. These kids wanted to live legally in the United States and go to school. He had proven unable to change their fate, but he might be able to do something for one of them. His staff contacted the United States Citizenship and Immigration Services and asked them to reconsider their stance on Oscar's application. Maybe it would make a difference.

In July 2010, Karla loaded her daughter, Samantha, into the car and backed out of the driveway. She had taken three days off to go see Oscar but stopped when she reached the road. She felt that she was forgetting something and glanced over at the mailbox. She hadn't checked it yet and decided to grab whatever was in there.

Amid a stack of overdue bills was an envelope from U.S. Immigration and Customs Enforcement. Confused, she opened it and read it twice before shoving it back in the envelope.

Karla took a deep breath, climbed back in the car, and set off on the four-hour drive to Magdalena. When she arrived, she wrapped her arms around Oscar.

He noticed that something was different. "What is it?"

"Let's unload the car."

"Just tell me."

"The car," Karla ordered.

Oscar dutifully unloaded the car and put Samantha down for a nap. When the room was quiet, Karla took out the letter and handed it to Oscar.

"What is it?"

"Read."

Oscar looked at her and then started reading: *Your application for permanent residency status in the United States of America has been approved.*

Oscar didn't react.

"You understand what this means, right?"

Oscar still couldn't say anything.

Karla took his hands. "It means you're coming home."

IN LATE AUGUST 2010, Oscar returned to the United States after a year in Mexico. The auto-parts company he was working for offered him a promotion and a raise if he'd stay in Magdalena. He politely declined.

Allan and Debbie threw Oscar a big welcome-home party in their backyard. Lorenzo and Luis brought the food. It was hot, so they decided on a cool, crisp menu: salads, a cheese platter, and melon-flavored water they made by floating sliced bits of cantaloupe in a jug. When they saw Oscar, they wondered if they should have brought carne asada instead. Oscar had gotten skinny living by himself. His cheeks had hollowed out and he'd lost the heft of the squad-leading cadet he once was. He didn't mind. He was just happy to be back.

Oscar's exile from the United States had drawn national media coverage and brought him to the attention of Bard, an S&P 500 company with twenty-one thousand employees that designs and manufactures health-care equipment. Initially, before Oscar was readmitted to the United States, a director of plant operations at Bard e-mailed him to talk about hiring him in Nogales, Mexico. But when he received residency, the company offered him work at its Phoenix office. Oscar would be helping to design lifesaving medical devices, such as stents and catheters. It seemed like a great opportunity.

But then, two months after his return, Oscar rode his bike by an armed-services recruiting office in a mall on East Baseline Road. He had learned to ignore the recruiting offices over the years, but now something clicked in his head.

"I can do that now," he thought. "I could enlist."

He rode his bike into the mall and stepped into the office. The recruiter was happy to see him. The Afghan War was still raging—the Army needed high-quality candidates like Oscar. He had a college degree and could apply for Officer Candidate School. It was a natural choice, but Oscar wasn't interested in starting out as an officer.

"I want to serve as a soldier," he told the recruiter. Oscar couldn't imagine ordering men into battle without having first experienced combat as a grunt. He wanted his authority to come from experience, not from some bars on his shoulders.

"You'd be entering as a specialist," the recruiter warned him. It was a harder path. Oscar would be starting from near the bottom of the military hierarchy and would have to work his way up the chain of command step-by-step. It could take years, but Oscar was accustomed to that. He didn't believe in shortcuts. He believed in hard work.

"That sounds great," he told the recruiter.

IN MAY 2011, Oscar was crawling through mud puddles at Fort Knox in Kentucky. He had completed basic training and was now training to be a cavalry scout. He was covered in slime and sweat. It was ninety degrees out and the humidity made it feel even worse.

Oscar couldn't have been happier. Since he'd joined ROTC as a freshman at Carl Hayden, he'd dreamed of joining the Army and proving that he deserved to be an American. As the other fifty-odd members of his platoon careened into the puddle beside him, the drill sergeant shouted Oscar's name. He wiggled out, ran over, and saluted his superior.

"Vazquez, clean up and report to the A.G.," the drill sergeant barked.

Oscar followed orders and presented himself at the Adjutant General building—the Army's human resources unit. He filed into a courtroom with six other cadets. A civilian judge was waiting. It was his U.S. citizenship ceremony.

"Raise your right hand," the judge instructed.

Oscar swelled with pride as he raised his hand. He was finally going to belong somewhere. But it was more than that too. He was becoming part of something bigger than himself: the Army, the country, and an idea about how people should live together.

"I hereby declare, on oath, that I absolutely and entirely renounce and abjure all allegiance and fidelity to any foreign prince, potentate, state, or sovereignty, of whom or which I have heretofore been a subject or citizen," Oscar said.

The oath is something that most Americans don't know. Those who were born in the country are not required to state it and, as a result, are typically unaware of the obligations of citizenship. Oscar had no such illusions. He understood every word of the oath.

"That I will support and defend the Constitution and laws of the United States of America against all enemies, foreign and domestic," he said. "That I will bear arms on behalf of the United States when required by the law."

On November 29, 2011, Oscar boarded a plane bound for Afghanistan. Karla and Samantha waved to him from the departure area. The departure was tough for Karla. She had just gotten used to having her husband home. She was also five months pregnant with their second child. But as much as she wanted him to take the offer from Bard, she wasn't surprised by Oscar's decision to enlist: "I knew what was going to happen as soon as he got back to the U.S. It was his dream."

Oscar was deployed to a remote outpost in the mountainous Paktia Province of eastern Afghanistan. The Army dubbed the place Firebase Wilderness, but the soldiers who lived there just called it Wild. It occupied the lowland in a steep ravine between mountains. To Oscar, it looked hard to defend as just about anybody in the mountains above could rain fire down on them.

It turned out he was right. Nearly every dawn, Taliban fighters launched rockets at the outpost. Oscar thought of it as their way of saying "Good morning." Just when he was getting used to the routine of outpost life, his platoon was sent into the mountains on a search-and-destroy mission. The goal was simple: find enemies and kill them.

The platoon hiked for five days through the mountains and saw nothing of note. They were tired from hoofing up and down the steep ravines with heavy packs and body armor. They were about to set up camp when a burst of gunfire ripped over their heads. They dove for cover and dug into the hillside. The Taliban did nothing all night. It was as if they wanted to wear the soldiers down with anticipation.

In the morning, Oscar and his platoon sergeant scrambled up the hill to set up an observation post. When they got to the top, a massive volley of fire tore up the ground around them. The firefight had begun.

"Return fire!" the platoon sergeant yelled.

It was Oscar's first combat experience, and he was worried that he would freeze. He had devoted years of his life to climbing ropes and doing push-ups as an ROTC cadet, all with the goal of fighting for the United States. He had deported himself from the country in order to have the honor of defending it someday. Now all those years of anticipation had coalesced. He flipped the safety off his M4 rifle and lit up the hill across the valley. Artillery shells exploded around him, covering him in dust. He repositioned and kept firing. He wasn't scared or worried anymore. As the enemy retreated, the firefight wound down, Oscar felt a sense of accomplishment.

"This is exactly what I wanted to do," he thought.

He was a true American combat soldier now.

IN THE FALL OF 2013, Hollywood began filming a movie about the Carl Hayden robotics team. It was a co-production between Lionsgate Entertainment and Grupo Televisa, the Mexican broadcasting company, and focused on the team's victory in Santa Barbara. The film ends when the awards for the 2004 MATE competition are announced. Just as the announcer in the real ceremony did a little drumroll on the podium before calling Carl Hayden to the stage, the actor playing the announcer also drums a podium. The actors playing the teenagers leap to their feet just as Oscar, Lorenzo, Cristian, and Luis leapt. It was the type of moment that feels like a fitting end to a movie.

In reality, life is more complicated. The attention paid to the team as a result of their victory coincided with a backlash against immigrants in Arizona. The state's voters passed propositions 200 and 300, making it more difficult for immigrants living in the country illegally to attend college. It had a direct impact on Oscar and Cristian, both of whom struggled to finish degrees. While Oscar ultimately graduated, Cristian did not.

The atmosphere in Phoenix became more polarized in the years following Stinky's victory. In 2008, Sheriff Joe Arpaio started saturation patrols of West Phoenix. He ordered officers into predominantly Latino neighborhoods and told them to enforce all traffic laws. The goal was to pull locals over for minor offenses, demand proof of citizenship or residency, and then deport anybody who was there illegally. Arpaio told CNN that he was able to determine someone's residency status by "their conduct, what type of clothes they're wearing, their speech."

Arpaio's actions drew the attention of the Justice Department, which launched a three-year investigation of the Maricopa County Sheriff's Office. Federal investigators determined that Arpaio's organization had "a pervasive culture of discriminatory bias against Latinos" that "reaches the highest levels of the agency." In 2011, the federal government revoked Arpaio's authority to identify and detain immigrants.

But that authority was explicitly granted to other members of law enforcement statewide by Arizona State Bill 1070, an effort to increase pressure on undocumented immigrants in the state to leave. Passed in 2010, it provided strict penalties for people who sheltered, hired, or transported unregistered immigrants and required local law enforcement officers to question individuals suspected of being in the country illegally. Though some provisions were struck down by the U.S. Supreme Court, key elements were upheld and the bill stands as one of the most aggressive measures to curtail undocumented immigration.

Nationwide, attitudes toward migrants have also proven increasingly divisive. Repeated efforts to pass immigration-reform bills in the House have failed, as conservatives argue that any effort to grant amnesty only rewards people who have broken the law. Similarly, the DREAM Act has stalled on arguments that allowing children who have illegally entered the United States to achieve legal residency as a result of attending school creates an added incentive for families to illegally enter the country. In June 2012, President Obama stoked conservative furor by issuing an executive order deferring for two years the deportation of immigrants who would have qualified for the DREAM Act had it passed. Lorenzo and Cristian applied for protection under the order and were granted so-called "deferred action." It bought them temporary safety, but the next president could quickly end the program.

Opponents of the DREAM Act view immigrants as competitors for finite American resources. "What will you say to an American kid who does not get into a state university and whose family cannot afford a private college because that seat and that subsidy have been given to someone who is in the country illegally?" asks Ira Mehlman, the media director for the Federation for American Immigration Reform, an organization that lobbies against the DREAM Act.

Some signs suggest that the vehemence of the anti-immigrant movement has driven migrants away. Statewide, enrollment in Arizona public schools has declined since the passage of anti-immigrant propositions 200 and 300. Some construction projects in Phoenix have reportedly slowed due to a lack of labor. To some, these are positive developments. "Arizona has been overwhelmed with illegal immigration and all the negative things that follow—crime, increased public service costs, especially education, and depression of our wages," said Arizona State Representative John Kavanagh. "Denying the in-state tuition, besides being fair to residents, also deters illegal immigrants from coming here."

The movie provides a happy ending. It's an ending that continues to elude some of the individuals portrayed in the story. In one of the final scenes, Esai Morales, the actor playing Lorenzo's dad, arrives at the MATE awards ceremony and sees his son win the national championship. The movie depicts their damaged relationship, how Lorenzo never felt loved by his father. I stood next to the real Lorenzo during the filming of the scene in Albuquerque, New Mexico. Lorenzo watched as José Julián, the actor playing him, catches sight of Morales and walks to him. Morales embraces Julián. Lorenzo and I watched waves of emotion pass across both actors' faces: pride, relief, and love. Lorenzo was transfixed.

"Cut!" the director suddenly shouted.

The actors wiped away tears, laughed, and drifted away.

Lorenzo and I remained standing at the edge of the banquet room.

Lorenzo stared at his feet. Finally, he glanced up at me and said quietly, trying not to cry, "My father would never do that."

TEN YEARS AFTER beating MIT, Lorenzo works as a line cook at St. Francis, an upscale restaurant in Phoenix. Oscar completed his tour of duty in Afghanistan and left the U.S. Army in June 2014 after achieving the rank of sergeant. He is now employed as a foreman in the locomotive shop at BNSF, the train company.

From 9:00 p.m. to 5:00 a.m., five nights a week, Luis empties trash cans at the federal courthouse in downtown Phoenix. On the weekends, he caters weddings, quinceañeras, and church retreats with Lorenzo.

Cristian continues to live at home and invent things in his room.

Fredi still teaches at Carl Hayden and coaches the robotics team. In 2011, 2012, 2013, and 2014, the team won the Arizona FIRST robotics championship. The team has collected top honors at regional, national, and international competitions, making it one of the most decorated programs in the country. Between 2002 and 2008, Fredi received no compensation for his work with the team. Starting in 2008, he was awarded three-fifths of a coaching stipend—roughly $240 a month.

Allan retired in 2006 and now volunteers his time to help the robotics team.

ACKNOWLEDGMENTS

Ten years ago, I flew to Phoenix to visit Carl Hayden Community High School and learn about its extraordinary robotics team. I was alerted to the students' accomplishments by Marcos Garcíaacosta, an Intel employee who was kind enough to write me. I am grateful he did.

My colleagues at *Wired* have been immensely supportive over the years. Federico Schott designed the original article, Livia Corona took amazing photos, and Zana Woods was the photo editor. Joanna Pearlstein ran fact-checking. Bob Cohn was the executive editor at the time and taught me a lot about being a journalist. Chris Anderson, the editor in chief from 2001 to 2012, gave me my start in journalism and sent me to Phoenix in 2005. Most important, Mark Robinson has been my longtime editor. He has read multiple drafts of almost everything I've written and made it better at every stage. He is a true mentor and friend.

My literary agent, Bonnie Nadell, believed in this story from the start and has been a relentless advocate. Sean McDonald, my editor at Farrar, Straus and Giroux, added keen insights. Kelly Vicars, my research assistant, was a great help during the intense writing period.

My friend Rick Jacobs at Circle of Confusion fought for a decade to turn this into a film, as did my lawyer, Keith Fleer, and film agent, Shari Smiley. I owe a debt of gratitude to George Lopez, Jamie Lee Curtis, Marisa Tomei, Carlos Pena, Alexa PenaVega, José Julián, Oscar Gutierrez, David Del Rio, Ben Odell, Sean McNamara, Elissa Matsueda, and David Alpert for bringing the film to life.

My wife and kids have put up with my reporting trips and long hours of writing. This book is a result of their support. Ben Peterson read an early draft and gave valuable feedback. I owe thanks as well to Joshuah Bearman, who picked up the slack at *Epic Magazine* while I was writing the book.

I want to recognize the great work that Jill Zande does at the

Marine Advanced Technology Education Center. She spearheaded the ROV competition and has inspired countless kids. Without her, the Carl Hayden team would not have had the opportunity to compete. Similarly, Ed Moriarty has built a phenomenal learning environment for budding engineers at MIT's Edgerton Center and gave me an enlightening tour.

Over a ten-year period, I returned frequently to Phoenix to interview Carl Hayden teachers and alums, all of whom were gracious and put up with my questions. Dulce Matuz, a Carl Hayden graduate, offered incisive perspectives on the immigration environment. Additionally, many young roboticists over the years have patiently explained their creations. Team 842 continues to inspire me.

My biggest debt of gratitude is to the members of the 2004 Carl Hayden underwater-robotics team and their families. The Arandas, Arcegas, Santillans, and Vazquezes welcomed me into their homes and talked to me countless times over the past decade, answering my incessant, persnickety questions with humor and patience.

The team's mentors and their families were also endlessly available to help me. Debbie Cameron and Pam Lajvardi graciously invited me into their homes and provided important insight. Finally, Allan Cameron and Fredi Lajvardi have devoted their lives to helping kids achieve their potential. This book is dedicated to them.

A Note About the Author

Joshua Davis has been a contributing editor at *Wired* for a decade and is the cofounder of *Epic Magazine*. He is the author of *The Underdog*, a memoir about his experiences as an arm wrestler, backward runner, and matador. In 2014, his work for *Wired* was nominated for a National Magazine Award for feature writing. He has also written for *The New Yorker* and other periodicals, and his writing is anthologized in the 2012 edition of *The Best American Science and Nature Writing*, as well as in the 2006, 2007, and 2009 editions of *The Best Technology Writing*. The movie *Spare Parts* is based on his reporting. He lives in San Francisco with his family.